COOKIES & BEER

ALSO BY
JONATHAN BENDER

LEGO: A LOVE STORY

TOGETHER AT LAST

COOKIES
&
BEER

BAKE • PAIR • ENJOY

JONATHAN BENDER
PHOTOGRAPHY BY RON BERG

Andrews McMeel
Publishing®

Kansas City • Sydney • London

CONTENTS

INTRODUCTION

"*Milk* is for babies. WHEN YOU GROW UP, you have to drink *beer.*"

ARNOLD SCHWARZENEGGER,
Pumping Iron

Cookies and beer. You just read that and smiled, right? I'm smiling, too, because this is a big, silly, wonderful idea.

This is fun. Real, good fun in the kitchen. And at the dining room table. And with friends and a sink full of empty glasses and plates with only crumbs on them.

It is happy conversation and unexpected discoveries. It's the fact that even when we failed to pair the right cookie with the right beer, the worst thing that happened was we had cookies and beer. This is the rare offer outside of an infomercial with no downside.

Good. Now that we've acknowledged that we're here for the fun, we can get down to the real work in the kitchen. This book is a blueprint—a way for you to begin appreciating two things you think you know about, but in an entirely new light. This is only the starting point, because it's probably going to take the forty cookie recipes that follow to find your own forever pairings.

As a journalist for the past fourteen years, I've had two guiding principles: unshakable optimism and a desire to make people care about a story even if they know nothing about the story's subject matter. The same principles underscore this (my first) cookbook. Whether you're a beer lover or the baker in your family, you'll find something new in these pages, and hopefully, you'll be both by the time you get to the end.

Cookies and beer are more connected than they might seem on the surface. They can share common grains, spices, and fruits. In the past five years, breweries have made liquid homages to oatmeal raisin cookies, chocolate chip cookies, and even Girl Scout cookies. And bakers have long known that beer can add unique flavor and depth to desserts that go beyond mere novelty.

This book actually began with an event. Cookies and Beer was going to be a one-night-only affair. It was a way to catch the attention of a city and announce that I had a new food writing project, *Recommended Daily*. We created four cookie and beer pairings, accompanied by tasting notes, and set up a table at Bier Station, a local beer bar/bottle shop. And then we sold more than 250 cookies in about forty-five minutes. Food lovers already knew what I was just learning—this was a winning combination.

Here is the secret to this book: The right beer and cookie pairing is outstanding because it allows you to enjoy more of both elements. Milk washes away or rounds off the edges of a cookie, but beer, the perfect beer, brings out something unexpected from the cookie or has its own lip-smacking revelation. Likewise, a great cookie can awaken flavors in a beer that you may have barely noticed before.

I wear the apron in my family, but I am no baker. So, I did what every food writer does when they need help in the kitchen—I asked the folks who do it for a living. I reached out to bakers (including Dolce Bakery's Erin Brown, who provided the first batch of cookies for the event that put us all on this journey), pastry chefs, and savory chefs with the request for a great cookie recipe that I could pair with beer. The responses from

places that regularly populate the lists of the nation's best cookies ensures that these cookies will wow you before you even take a sip of the accompanying beer.

Once the recipes started arriving, I got out the cherry red stand mixer that I had never used in a decade of marriage, and, as I had with our electric drill, I learned how to use it while keeping my fingers mostly intact. And then I used my own palate—I've been a beer writer for the past four years—to give each of these recipes a specific beer pairing, as well as a suggested beer style in case that recommended beer isn't available where you live.

Since I know this may very well be your first time trying cookies and beer together, I organized the book to help you (and your palate) adjust to the idea. The book begins with cookies like the **BACON CHIP SUGAR BOMBS** (page 17) that evoke breakfast. Think rich and salty and fatty—familiar flavors that make you want to reach for a beer. Just as bakers may be new to drinking beer, I know that beer drinkers may have never donned an apron. You also may not always have the time or inclination to bake. For those new to baking or those who simply love Oreos, I've got you covered with the section on PACKAGED COOKIES & BEER (page 19).

After that, you'll wade into a well-established category of pairing—chocolate and beer—discovering how combinations like **CHOCOLATE-ALMOND-COCONUT MACAROONS** (page 33) and Avery Brewing Company's The Reverend can call to mind a chocolate-covered cherry. At this point, you'll be ready for me to hand over the keys. And if Thin Mints are an annual spring tradition in your family, you'll want to flip to the section covering GIRL SCOUT COOKIES & BEER (page 40).

The cookies speak for themselves, but they are also holding a conversation with the beer. So, let's get you fluent in both halves of the dialogue. In the FRUIT chapter (page 41), you'll start to see how cookies can highlight elements in brews that you never expected. And now that you'll start having more beer in the house, I'll also show you what to do with that last bottle in the six-pack with a recipe for beer syrup that rehabilitates the BEER MILK SHAKE (page 57).

The final three sections are where you can earn your master's in pairing cookies and beer. Imagine if they offered that class in college. The SAVORY (page 59) section showcases the herb and spice notes that are becoming the hallmark of craft brewers. Then you'll dive into baking with SPENT GRAINS (page 87)—beer's grain by-product and the tastiest recycling you'll ever encounter. In the end, our two worlds meet in one delicious circle: cookies made with beer. Beer can be a beautiful ingredient in the right hands and the right cookie.

This is a guidebook for a new way to enjoy dessert. It's not just milk that might be replaced. You may also find yourself reaching for the beer list instead of asking for port or dessert wine. Beer is the best thing to happen to cookies since Ruth Graves Wakefield broke up pieces of chocolate and created the first chocolate chips in 1938. Enjoy cookies and beer. They were meant to be together.

FOR BAKERS NEW TO DRINKING BEER

With a plethora of beers on the market, it's easy to feel overwhelmed by the sheer volume of choices. But don't be intimidated, because, as a wise bartender once told me, "Nobody is born liking beer." Ask lots of questions. Empty lots of glasses. Pour a few you don't like down the drain. And never let anybody tell you what you like is wrong.

It can take a while to find the beer you love, but the joy of that eventual discovery is worth the effort. The cookies in this book will help you find something unexpected in beer and also show you how it can be a great complement to what you're eating. As part of that journey, here's a primer on the hoppy stuff if you don't regularly have a six-pack in your fridge.

BEER IS A SUBTLE INGREDIENT

When it comes to baking with beer, the actual flavor imparted by the brew is more subtle than you think. None of the cookies are boozy or bitter because of the beer involved. Often, the beer provides depth or balances out the sweetness of sugar in a way that you may sense rather than explicitly taste.

WALK TOWARD THE LIGHT AND DARK

Let's stick with color for classifying beers. Blonde, golden, and wheat (Hefeweizen is the German-style wheat) are beers on the lighter end of the spectrum. Amber and brown are square in the middle. Porters, stouts, and dark ales are typically inky, opaque affairs. One style of beer that deserves a quick, separate mention is India pale ales. IPAs'

A GUIDE TO
BEER
GLASSES

GOBLET: Belgian strong dark ale, quadrupel

SNIFTER: imperial stout, barrel-aged brews

OVERSIZED WINE GLASS: Belgian ales

TULIP: farmhouse ale, imperial IPAs

MUG (OR STEIN): stout, porter

PINT GLASS (OR TUMBLER): oatmeal stout, brown

STANGE (SLENDER CYLINDER): Kölsch, lambic

PILSNER: pilsner, maibock

WEIZEN: wheat, Hefeweizen

intensity depends on the amount and type of hops—the flowers of the hop plant that can lend a piney or citrusy bent to a brew. If you hate IPAs, give it two years and try again.

These are general categories, but the good news is that beer makers will tell you when something is unusual—a dark brew with a light taste or body—because it's how they make their beers stand out.

A SURPRISE IN EVERY BOTTLE

If you stopped drinking beer in college and think of craft beer simply as a stronger version of the stuff in a keg you never really liked, you're in for a happy surprise. Beer can be spicy and sweet or salty and sour. Beer can taste like coffee and candy and chocolate milk.

In order to navigate all those flavors, here are some potential starting points. Coffee drinkers are built for a dry stout, red wine drinkers will be drawn to Flemish sours, white wine drinkers who like fruit can hunt down a Belgian tripel, and those who prefer a drier white might opt for a saison. Bourbon and whiskey drinkers go find the words "barrel-aged" on a bottle. And everyone should drink a radler—a mixture of beer and sparkling soda—in the summertime.

BEER GONE BAD

Like spoiled milk, beer has off flavors to warn you if it has gone bad. You may smell or taste buttered popcorn, cabbage, cardboard, or green apple. That is the beer letting you know something's not right. If your beer is flat or gushes out of the bottle when you pop the top, let it go.

FOR BEER DRINKERS NEW TO BAKING

Baking is more similar to drinking than you might first imagine. Both require dedication, a bit of practice, mistakes that you only confess to your loved ones, and a willingness to experiment on occasion.

Cookies are the best way to enter the world of baking. You can produce something incredible without a lot of effort, or even skill, because you're piggybacking on the experience of bakers and pastry chefs. Once you start baking, you'll discover that all ovens are different and you should trust your eyes and fingers when checking if a cookie is done. But while you're learning, cookies come with a built-in second chance. If you burn or undercook the first set, there's usually a second baking sheet waiting to go in the oven. You just have to own (or borrow) a few specific kitchen tools and pay attention to a few key ingredients.

TAKE A STAND MIXER

You'll need a stand mixer—it's the primary-colored behemoth from your wedding registry that you use intermittently. It's essential in cookie making, so dig it out or borrow a friend's mixer.

MEASURE UP

Baking, like beer brewing, is about accuracy. You must possess a full coterie of measuring cups (wet and dry are not the same) and spoons. These are wildly inexpensive and available everywhere from IKEA to Target to the dollar store. If you're measuring out spices and dry ingredients like flour or sugar, gently fill a measuring cup or spoon (unless told to pack the cup firmly). Then, level the top with the straight edge of a butter knife.

ALL THE BUTTER

The forty recipes in *Cookies & Beer* call for somewhere between thirty and three million sticks of butter. Julia Child once said, "With enough butter, anything is good," which makes this cookbook right here great.

Butter is one of those make-or-break ingredients for cookies because the way it is used and its temperature have a direct impact on the texture and flavor of what you're making. That's why you'll have to cube it with a knife, brown it on the stove, and cream it with sugar. Just think of your increased butter consumption as a way to say sorry to cows for trading in milk for beer.

BREAK THE CHOCOLATE BANK

Butter is often the reason something tastes amazing. It's the reason you make that "oh my goodness" face every time you bite into a pastry. The other most common reason: great chocolate.

Quality chocolate is expensive, but in this instance, it's worth the hit to your account balance. Great chocolate makes cookies sing and takes them from something you sacrifice to the office kitchen (where taste is less important than the fact that they exist) to something that makes you a boss.

THROW ON AN APRON

Flour is like beach sand: You'll never leave the kitchen without a bit on you. Therefore, this is your chance to don an apron. You can make a statement like your favorite bumper sticker or simply look the part of a baker (which is half the trick).

BREAKFAST

MAN BARS • 3

MAPLE TOASTED
OATMEAL COOKIES • 6

BACON SHORTBREAD
COOKIES • 8

OATMEAL COOKIES
WITH CHOCOLATE AND
CRANBERRIES • 10

BACON PECAN SANDIES • 12

OATMEAL COOKIES • 14

BACON CHIP
SUGAR BOMBS • 17

"Great cookies have a great texture—not too *soft*, not too brittle—and have a deep or distinct flavor. What makes them **STAND OUT** from other desserts is that they're not just *dessert*—they're snacks and treats and **SOMETIMES BREAKFAST**."

STACY BEGIN, co-owner,
Two Fat Cats Bakery

The right breakfast is a Las Vegas buffet. You've got crunchy and salty and sweet and more than you could ever finish in one sitting. The maple and oatmeal–inspired cookies in this chapter, such as the BACON SHORTBREAD COOKIES (page 8), evoke breakfast with every bite. And they want BREWS WITH GRAPEFRUIT AND ROASTY COFFEE NOTES that would be right at home at the breakfast table.

The diet of a newspaperman is what keeps cardiologists in business. In a small news bullpen just outside of Boston, I learned that pork steaks, Philly cheesesteaks, and day-old pizza from the trunk of a retired cop's car could all be considered breakfast in a pinch. It was there that I also discovered that a coffee shop will sell you a cookie in the morning without blinking. And lo, I thought I invented breakfast cookies. Turns out, we'll all sneak a cookie in the morning if there's a full cookie jar on the counter. Life is about more than breakfast for dinner. Sometimes, you have to have dessert for breakfast.

MAN BARS

STEPHANIE DIAZ, Sweetness Bake Shop & Café
Miami, Florida

Just out of the oven, these cookie bars smell like soft-baked pretzels. And they're the ballpark pretzels you really want (even without any actual pretzels in them)—a little sweet because of the butter and brown sugar, a little crunchy thanks to the chips and bacon with these tiny bursts of salt. The only thing missing from this recipe is your couch.

After a bite of the rich bar, the oatmeal stout is like a cool mug of creamy diner coffee. The bar brings out the roasty malt notes in the brew and the chocolate in the beer's nose finds a great partner in the breadlike cookies. Dunking is encouraged.

MAKES: 24 cookies
PAIRING: Samuel Smith's Oatmeal Stout
STYLE: An oatmeal stout has some big notes of coffee and caramel that match up nicely with the salty side of these cookie bars.

Butter, for the pan

2 cups all-purpose flour

1 teaspoon baking powder

¼ teaspoon fine sea salt

½ cup (1 stick) unsalted butter, melted

2 cups firmly packed light brown sugar

2 large eggs, at room temperature

2 tablespoons stout beer

1 cup kettle chips, crushed (see Note)

¼ cup chopped cooked applewood smoked bacon

NOTE: Put the potato chips in a resealable plastic bag and crush them gently with your hands before you measure them.

Preheat the oven to 350°F. Grease a 9 by 13-inch baking pan with butter or line it with parchment paper.

In a medium bowl, whisk together the flour, baking powder, and salt. Set aside.

In the bowl of a stand mixer fitted with the paddle attachment, or in a large bowl using a hand mixer, beat together the butter and brown sugar on medium-high speed until smooth, light, and fluffy.

CONTINUED ⟶

MAN BARS

With the mixer on low speed, add the eggs one at a time, waiting until the first is fully incorporated before adding the next.

Add the beer and mix on medium speed until the color of the batter is uniform. Add the flour mixture, potato chips, and bacon. Mix until combined.

Pour the batter into the prepared pan and smooth the top with a spatula. Bake for 20 to 25 minutes, until the top is golden brown. Let cool completely, then cut into bars.

The cookies will keep in an airtight container at room temperature for up to 4 days, or in the freezer for up to 1 month.

NOTE: You can replace potato chips and bacon with salty (pretzels, pecans) or sweet (chocolate or butterscotch chips) ingredients.

MAPLE TOASTED
OATMEAL COOKIES

ERIN BROWN, Dolce Bakery
Prairie Village, Kansas

This one is like the genie in *Aladdin*—all the best parts of breakfast in an itty-bitty bite. The brown sugar and maple syrup come together with the toasted oats like a warm bowl of storybook porridge.

No breakfast is complete without a cup of joe, and the porter gives you the roasty warmness of coffee. It's got warmth and depth without bitterness, lending the cookie a touch of creaminess.

MAKES: 24 cookies
PAIRING: Martin City Brewing Company's Robust Porter
STYLE: Baltic porter has smoke and roasted notes that bring out the maple goodness in the cookies and pair naturally with the sugar and oatmeal.

¾ cup (1½ sticks) unsalted butter, at room temperature, divided, plus 2 tablespoons, melted

2 cups old-fashioned rolled oats

1½ cups quick-cooking oats

1¼ cups all-purpose flour

1 teaspoon baking soda

1 teaspoon fine sea salt

1 cup firmly packed light brown sugar

1 teaspoon vanilla extract

1 tablespoon molasses

¼ cup maple syrup

½ cup granulated sugar

1 large egg

1 large egg yolk

Preheat the oven to 300°F. Line a rimmed baking sheet with parchment paper.

In a medium bowl, toss the 2 tablespoons melted butter with the oats. Spread the oats evenly with a spatula on the prepared baking sheet. Toast in the oven for 5 minutes. Toss gently with a spatula. Toast for 5 minutes more. Set aside and let cool.

While the oats are toasting, in a medium skillet, melt 6 tablespoons of the butter over medium heat. Once it stops sizzling, swirl the pan until the butter smells nutty and brown bits form on the bottom. Once the bits are amber, 2½ to 3 minutes after the sizzling stops, remove the butter from the heat and pour into a small bowl to cool.

In a large bowl, combine the toasted oats, quick-cooking oats, flour, baking soda, and salt. Set aside.

In the bowl of a stand mixer fitted with the paddle attachment, cream together the remaining 6 tablespoons butter and the brown sugar on low to medium speed until smooth. Beat in the vanilla, molasses, and maple syrup. Add the cooled browned butter and the granulated sugar and beat until the dough is uniform. Beat for 1 to 2 minutes on low to medium speed, until smooth and fluffy. Add the egg and egg yolk and mix until combined.

With the mixer on low speed, add the oat mixture in four increments. Mix only until the oat mixture is incorporated. Cover the mixing bowl with plastic wrap and refrigerate for at least 30 minutes.

Preheat the oven to 350°F. Line two baking sheets with parchment paper.

Scoop 1½ to 2-tablespoon balls of the dough onto the prepared baking sheet. Space them 2 inches apart and flatten them slightly with a fork or your palm.

Bake for 6 minutes, then rotate the baking sheet 180 degrees and bake for 6 to 7 minutes more. The cookies should be light golden brown in color. Let cool for at least 5 minutes on the baking sheet.

The cookies will keep in an airtight container at room temperature for up to 3 days.

BACON SHORTBREAD COOKIES

ABBEY-JO AND JOSH EANS, Happy Gillis
Kansas City, Missouri

Donald Trump would say this cookie is rich. The bacon grease and butter form a lovely undercurrent that gives the shortbread depth, like eggs cooked in the same pan as your slab bacon. The bacon bits are tiny salty bonus bites providing a nice textural balance to the soft slices.

Stiegl Radler and this cookie are like brunch and dessert had a baby. "Bressert" starts with that rich bacon and then this big, juicy grapefruit half arrives to refresh your palate. The beer's carbonation and light citrus make the cookie crackle like a righteous piece of buttered toast.

MAKES: 48 cookies
PAIRING: Stiegl Radler
STYLE: Radlers have a long tradition in Germany. The equal portions of beer and citrus soda or juice are great complements to rich and fatty foods and desserts.

15 slices bacon

1½ cups (3 sticks) unsalted butter, at room temperature

2 cups granulated sugar

¾ cup firmly packed light brown sugar

4 teaspoons kosher salt

6 large egg yolks

½ cup vanilla extract

7½ cups all-purpose flour

In a griddle or cast-iron pan, cook the bacon over medium-low heat until just crispy. Pour the grease off into a glass measuring cup and set aside to cool. You will need 1½ cups of the bacon fat for the cookies. Break the bacon into small pieces.

In the bowl of a stand mixer fitted with the paddle attachment, cream together 1½ cups of the cooled bacon fat, the butter, granulated sugar, brown sugar, and salt on medium speed. Once the mixture is uniform, lower the mixer speed to low and add the egg yolks one at a time. Add the vanilla. Scrape down the sides of the bowl and paddle attachment. With the mixer running on low speed, slowly add the flour. Once the mixture starts to come together, add the bacon pieces and mix on low for about a minute, until the bacon is incorporated.

Place a pair of plastic wrap sheets on a flat surface. Separate the dough into two even logs, about 12 inches long and between 2 and 3 inches high. Wrap the dough in the plastic wrap and refrigerate for at least 2 hours, until firm. The dough will keep in the fridge for 1 week or in the freezer for 1 month.

Preheat the oven to 325°F. Line a pair of baking sheets with parchment paper.

Slice the chilled dough logs into ¼-inch-thick slices and place them ½ inch apart on the prepared baking sheets. Bake for 10 minutes, or until the cookies have a matte finish and a light golden color around the base. If the cookies are shiny, they're not done. The cookies will keep in an airtight container at room temperature for 2 to 4 days.

OATMEAL COOKIES WITH
CHOCOLATE AND CRANBERRIES

JEFF USINOWICZ, corporate executive chef
Deschutes Brewery, Bend, Oregon

The key to a beautiful Thanksgiving sandwich is a healthy dollop of sweet-and-tart cranberry sauce or relish. The same holds true with this cookie, where bright red sparks of cranberry make the chocolate dance on your tongue, lighten up the oatmeal, and cleanse your palate. It's a lot of work for a little bit of berry.

The malt in the Mirror Pond skates alongside the sweetened oatmeal, helping the cinnamon and nutmeg come out in the cookie. The tart cranberry grabs the citrus and fruit notes in the beer and pulls up them like the claw in a Big Choice machine.

MAKES: 48 cookies
PAIRING: Deschutes Brewery's Mirror Pale Pond Ale
STYLE: A medium-bodied amber ale or American pale ale will lend fruit or hop notes (think floral or piney) that complement the cookie.

Butter, for the pan

1¼ cups old-fashioned rolled oats

1¼ cups all-purpose flour

¾ cup granulated sugar

½ cup firmly packed dark brown sugar

¼ teaspoon freshly grated nutmeg

¼ teaspoon ground cinnamon

½ teaspoon baking soda

¼ teaspoon fine sea salt

10 tablespoons (1¼ sticks) unsalted butter, at room temperature

1 large egg

1 teaspoon vanilla extract

1 cup milk chocolate or dark chocolate chips

½ cup coarsely chopped fresh or frozen cranberries

Preheat the oven to 350°F. Grease a pair of baking sheets with butter.

In a large bowl, use a wooden spoon or spatula to mix together the oats, flour, granulated sugar, brown sugar, nutmeg, cinnamon, baking soda, and salt until thoroughly combined. Add the butter, egg, and vanilla and mix for 2 to 3 minutes, until the batter is even in color. Fold in the chocolate and cranberries.

Drop tablespoons of the dough about 2 inches apart on the baking sheets. Bake for 13 to 15 minutes, until the edges begin to turn golden brown. Let cool for 10 minutes on the baking sheet, or until the cookies easily slide off the baking sheet. The cookies will keep in an airtight container at room temperature for up to 1 week.

PECAN SANDIES

AMY EMBERLING, managing partner
Zingerman's Bakehouse, Ann Arbor, Michigan

We should all be lucky to spend a summer at Camp Bacon, the annual pork-themed celebration held every June at Zingerman's. It's there that the good folks of Ann Arbor, Michigan, delve into sweet and savory bacon dishes, attend cooking classes, and essentially give themselves over to fatty pork belly—and have been doing so since long before such a thing was trendy.

For the first time, you can have a little bit of Camp Bacon in your home. Zingerman's Bakehouse managing partner Amy Emberling thought the "brown sugar nature of the pecan sandy would be well suited with the smoky bacon." You'll agree wholeheartedly. The toasted pecans and salty bacon elevate this classic cookie into bites that will leave you unintentionally and audibly moaning.

The savory elements in the bacon pecan sandy sing with your first sip of Founders Porter. The cookie becomes richer—the toasted pecans acting like high-class nuts on the end of the bar. And the salt of the bacon dances with the caramel malts in the porter, leaving you with a liquid version of salted caramel.

MAKES: 24 cookies
PAIRING: Founders Brewing Co. Porter
STYLE: Porters have a great way of enhancing the sweet and salty notes in the cookie without throwing off the balance of the contrasting elements.

1 cup (2 sticks) unsalted butter, at room temperature

½ cup granulated sugar

2 teaspoons vanilla extract

5 or 6 slices bacon, cooked

2 cups all-purpose flour

1 cup pecan pieces, toasted

Pinch of coarse sea salt (optional)

1 to 2 tablespoons Demerara sugar, for sprinkling (optional)

Preheat the oven to 325°F. Line a pair of baking sheets with waxed paper or silicone mats.

In a large bowl, use a wooden spoon or a hand mixer to cream together the butter and sugar. Add the vanilla and 2 teaspoons water and cream together. Chop the bacon into pieces a little bit bigger than a chocolate chip. Add the flour, pecans, and bacon and mix until incorporated.

> "I prefer **MY COOKIES** on the smaller side. I think they look cuter. I CAN'T RESIST little cookies."

AMY EMBERLING,
Zingerman's Bakehouse

Form the dough into 24 balls of the same size and place them on the prepared baking sheets. Press down on each ball using your palm or the bottom of a glass. Lightly sprinkle the tops of the cookies with coarse salt, Demerara sugar, or a combination of the two.

Bake for 22 to 24 minutes. The cookies will take on a light brown color. Remove from the oven and let cool.

The cookies will keep in an airtight container at room temperature for about 1 week.

oatmeal cookies

TREY WINKLE, R Bar & Grill
Tulsa, Oklahoma

The first bite of this cookie makes you think about how it would be a great foundation for an ice cream sandwich with sea salt caramel ice cream, or dipped in a jar of peanut butter like an edible spoon. By the second bite, you'll forget about doctoring it up and instead enjoy the cinnamon-y crunch that is reminiscent of breakfast cereal at the moment when it has soaked up milk but not yet gotten soggy.

This cookie wants a delicate brew, something a bit lighter that can add some spice notes without washing away the cookie. The oats in the cookie find the oats in the beer, but it's the coriander and orange peel (typically found in Belgian beers) that add some nice complexity to the pair.

MAKES: 24 cookies
PAIRING: Marshall Brewing Company's Sundown Wheat
STYLE: Wheat or summer ale. Look for summer brews that have citrus notes on the label or add a lemon or orange slice to your glass of wheat beer.

2 cups all-purpose flour

1 teaspoon baking soda

2 teaspoons kosher salt

1 teaspoon ground cinnamon

1 cup (2 sticks) unsalted butter, at room temperature

1 cup granulated sugar

1 cup firmly packed dark brown sugar

2 large eggs, at room temperature

3 cups quick-cooking oats

In a medium bowl, stir together the flour, baking soda, salt, and cinnamon with a whisk. Set aside.

In the bowl of a stand mixer fitted with the paddle attachment, cream together the butter, granulated sugar, and brown sugar on medium speed for 5 to 7 minutes, until very well combined. With the mixer running, add the eggs one at a time, waiting until the first is fully incorporated before adding the next, 2 to 3 minutes per egg.

With the mixer running on medium speed, gradually add the flour mixture. Beat for 5 minutes.

Fold in the oats by hand with a spatula until fully combined. Cover the bowl with plastic wrap and refrigerate for at least 1 hour, but not more than 12 hours.

"A great cookie, to me, is completely subjective. I think **EVERYONE HAS THEIR OWN PREFERENCE**. While some agree with soft in the middle and crispy edges, others believe it should snap, and some would rather eat the raw dough itself. Personally, I LOVE THE SLIGHTLY BROWNED, CRISPED EDGE while the rest of the cookie has a bite with no sound. That's the best way I can describe it."

TREY WINKLE,
R Bar & Grill

Preheat the oven to 350°F. Line a pair of baking sheets with parchment paper.

Use an ice cream scoop to measure out 2-ounce portions of dough (a little bigger than a Ping-Pong ball) and place them 1½ inches apart on the prepared baking sheets. Bake for 10 to 12 minutes, until the cookies have a crispy ring around the edge.

These cookies are best eaten right away, but will keep in an airtight container at room temperature for 3 to 5 days.

BACON CHIP SUGAR BOMBS

NICK WESEMANN, pastry chef, The American Restaurant
Kansas City, Missouri

This cookie has an unforgettable texture—it will be a benchmark for other cookies in your life. The unrefined sugar lends crunchiness to the silky inside, while the bacon's smokiness and saltiness volley and serve with the bittersweet chocolate. This is the bacon dessert you were promised, America.

The tart cherry lambic supercharges the sweetness in this cookie—your taste buds will be spinning around the room like a toddler after a sip of soda. The cherry brew also marries with the chocolate in the cookie, while the dry, sparkly finish cleanses your palate.

MAKES: 24 cookies
PAIRING: Lindemans Kriek
STYLE: For those with a sweet tooth, look for a fruit lambic (a traditional Belgian brew). If you're willing to experiment, try a tart sour beer to cut through the rich bacon and chocolate.

---

8 slices bacon

1¼ cups old-fashioned rolled oats

1 cup (2 sticks) plus 1 tablespoon unsalted butter

1⅓ cups firmly packed light brown sugar

1¼ cups turbinado sugar (such as Sugar in the Raw)

1 large egg

1 teaspoon vanilla extract

1¾ cups all-purpose flour

1 teaspoon baking soda

1 teaspoon kosher salt

1⅓ cups chopped bittersweet chocolate or chocolate chips

Line a baking sheet with parchment paper. Cook the bacon on a griddle over low heat until crispy. Transfer the bacon to a paper towel–lined plate to drain and cool. When cool, finely chop and set aside. Discard the fat in the pan.

Spread the oats on the prepared baking sheet and dot 1 tablespoon of the butter on top of the oats. Toast in the oven for 15 minutes, stirring the oats every 5 minutes. Let cool. In a food processor, pulse the cooled oats until they resemble coarse sand.

CONTINUED ▸→

BACON CHIP
SUGAR BOMBS

CONTINUED

In the bowl of a stand mixer fitted with the paddle attachment, cream together the brown sugar, turbinado sugar, and the remaining 1 cup butter. Scrape down the sides of the bowl and add the egg and vanilla. Mix until the egg is fully incorporated. On low speed, add the flour, baking soda, and salt. Mix until almost combined, then add the bacon, oats, and chocolate. Mix until the dough comes together. Remove the dough from the bowl and wrap it in plastic wrap. Refrigerate until firm, at least 1 hour.

Preheat the oven to 350°F. Line a baking sheet with parchment paper.

Use an ice cream scoop to measure out 1½- to 2-ounce portions of dough (a little bigger than a Ping-Pong ball) and place them at least 2 inches apart on the baking sheet. Bake for 12 minutes, or until golden brown. Transfer to a wire rack to cool.

The cookies will keep in an airtight container at room temperature for 5 to 7 days.

PACKAGED COOKIES & BEER

The Boston Sail Loft Café & Bar in Boston's North End has a gorgeous view of the Atlantic Ocean and a fine cup of New England clam chowder, but when I lived in the neighborhood, I went there for one reason alone: In the middle of the wooden bar that runs the length of the place, there is a glass cookie jar with a silver top. That jar is filled with Oreos, and the Oreos are free.

This was my favorite bar snack (and occasional dinner) in Beantown. I'd ask for a pint of Harpoon IPA and then eat more of the black and white sandwich cookies than I'd ever admit in print. Whether it was the beginning of the night or the end, I was always glad to see that big glass jar.

You may not always have time to bake, but that doesn't mean you should deprive yourself or your guests of experiencing cookies and beer. In the spirit of the Sail Loft, here are a few pairings of packaged cookies to get you started. After that, just take a shot with what's in your fridge and pantry—you may just find the next great combo.

GRAHAM CRACKERS & VANILLA PORTER: The mildness of the graham cracker requires a beer that won't overpower it. Enter the vanilla porter, which brings a bit of vanilla to play off the cinnamon or honey, and slightly amplifies the molasses in the graham cracker.

OREOS & MILK STOUT: You want to dunk Oreos. I get it. I do too. Milk stouts have the right amount of body and a hint of sweetness that doesn't get in the way of what Oreos are bringing to the table. Bonus: You can still get a milk stout mustache with very little effort.

PINWHEELS & IMPERIAL STOUT: This one is like campfire s'mores. It's warming and cozy and what you'll want to eat from now until the end of time. The roasty malts in the beer set off the chocolate, and the marshmallow comes in all gooey at the end. The combination is beer and cookies at its best, elevating both parts of the pairing.

VANILLA WAFERS & BOURBON BARREL-AGED BEER: Sometimes beer geeks will use vanilla wafers as a way to describe the toasty vanilla flavor of a brew. In this case, the vanilla notes of the bourbon barrel–aged brews enhance the cookie's toasty nature. The barrel-aging process allows beer to pick up the vanilla and natural fruit overtones that highlight the vanilla wafer.

GINGERBREAD MEN & AMERICAN-STYLE BARLEYWINE: The citrus of the hops in the beer cuts through the sharp bite of the ginger. The sugar from the cookie in turn melds with the notes of toffee, caramel, and oak that are commonly found in barleywines. As the beer warms and you take more bites, you'll keep finding those nuanced flavors in this silky partnership.

CHOCOLATE

MEXICAN HOT CHOCOLATE
COOKIES • 23

PEARL BAKERY CHOCOLATE CHUNK
COOKIES • 26

CHOCOLATE OATMEAL ALE COOKIES
WITH CARAMEL ICING • 28

CHEF AMY'S
CHOCOLATE CHIP COOKIE • 30

CHOCOLATE-ALMOND-COCONUT
MACAROONS • 33

CHOCOLATE-COVERED
CARAMEL-FILLED
SHORTBREAD COOKIES • 35

VALRHONA CHOCOLATE CHIP
COOKIES • 38

"Freshly baked **COOKIES** smell like the *warmth* and *safety* of childhood."

EMILY STONE, head pastry chef
Pearl Bakery

Chocolate and beer is one of the few pairings that has been oft explored, and the results can be dynamite. Just like the MEXICAN HOT CHOCOLATE COOKIES (page 23) have their heat tamed by a SMOKED PORTER, the key is to find complementary flavors. The sweetness in chocolate can amplify any bitterness present in a beer. But a bit of citrus or caramel can turn chocolate and beer into two comfortable slippers you'll want to wear all evening.

When I was in grade school, my grandmother would "hide" the chocolate chip cookies she made for me on top of my grandfather's dresser in their bedroom. He never opened the tin and pilfered a cookie because he always knew that I would sneak him a few while he sat in his recliner in the living room. These chocolate cookie recipes produce desserts worthy of theft. But they're even better when shared.

MEXICAN
hot chocolate cookies

ANNE NG, Bakery Lorraine
San Antonio, Texas

This cookie exists because a Texas bakery wanted its own version of a snickerdoodle. Inspiration arrived in the form of Mexican hot chocolate on a rainy day. There's an explosion of cinnamon and this rolling, blossoming heat from the habanero sugar that both work to show off the cookie's embodiment of drinking chocolate.

Where there is heat, you sometimes could use a bit of smoke. The smoked porter highlights the cinnamon and adds an exquisite roundness to the chocolate underneath. The effect lets your mouth sit comfortable in the eye of this tasty, spicy storm.

MAKES: 28 cookies
PAIRING: O'Fallon Brewery's Smoked Porter
STYLE: Smoked porters will tame the heat of this cookie and let that rich cinnamon and cocoa come to the forefront.

COOKIES

5 cups all-purpose flour

1½ cups unsweetened Dutch-process cocoa powder

½ tablespoon baking soda

½ tablespoon kosher salt

2½ tablespoons ground cinnamon

2 cups (4 sticks) plus 2 tablespoons unsalted butter, at room temperature

2 cups plus 2 tablespoons firmly packed dark brown sugar

1¾ cups granulated sugar

4 large eggs

2 cups semisweet chocolate chips

Preheat the oven to 325°F. Line two baking sheets with parchment paper.

To make the cookies, in a large bowl, combine the flour, cocoa, baking soda, salt, and cinnamon. Set aside.

In the bowl of a stand mixer fitted with the paddle attachment, cream together the butter, brown sugar, and granulated sugar on low to medium speed until light and fluffy. With the mixer running on low, add the eggs one at a time. Scrape down the bowl and make sure the eggs have been fully incorporated.

With the mixer running on low, add the flour mixture in a few batches. Mix until the dough looks smooth and even. Add the chocolate chips and mix on low just until the chips are evenly distributed.

CONTINUED ▸→

MEXICAN HOT CHOCOLATE COOKIES

CONTINUED

COATING

2 tablespoons habanero sugar (sold at specialty spice shops and online)

6 tablespoons granulated sugar

To make the coating, in a flat-bottomed bowl, combine the habanero sugar and the granulated sugar.

Use a ¼-cup or 2-ounce scoop to portion out the dough. Dredge the dough portions through the coating sugar, making sure to cover all sides. Place the cookies at least 3 inches apart on the prepared baking sheets.

Bake the cookies for 7 minutes, then rotate the pan 180 degrees and bake for 5 to 7 minutes more. The cookies are done when the edges are firm and the centers are still a little bit gooey.

The cookies will keep in an airtight container at room temperature for 2 to 3 days.

PEARL BAKERY
CHOCOLATE CHUNK COOKIES

EMILY STONE, Pearl Bakery
Portland, Oregon

On Saturday afternoons, once I got done playing youth soccer, my favorite treat was a sandy chocolate chip cookie with a huge glass of orange juice from a local bagel shop. The cold juice teased out the saltiness and was a great contrast in texture to the crumbly cookie wrapped in waxed paper. Pearl Bakery has managed to re-create that interplay of citrus and chocolate in a packed cookie that still feels light because of the fragrant orange zest.

Complex cookies are like high-energy dogs—they really need a beer that can keep up. The slight bitterness of the porter plays off the chocolate chunks. The chocolate, in turn, brings out beautiful roasted, malty flavors akin to a dark roast coffee in the beer.

MAKES: 24 cookies
PAIRING: Fuller's London Porter
STYLE: Opt for a robust English porter. The dark brew is light on hops but just right on body—perfect for the chocolate and citrus notes in this cookie.

3 cups all-purpose flour

¼ teaspoon baking soda

1 cup (2 sticks) unsalted butter, at room temperature

1½ cups firmly packed light brown sugar

1 teaspoon salt

Finely grated zest of 1 large orange

1 large egg

2 teaspoons vanilla extract (Mexican vanilla recommended)

1 cup pecan halves, lightly toasted

2 cups semisweet or bittersweet chocolate chunks

Preheat the oven to 350°F.

In a medium bowl, sift or whisk together the flour and baking soda. Set aside.

In the bowl of a stand mixer fitted with the paddle attachment, cream together the butter, brown sugar, salt, and orange zest on medium speed until light and fluffy, about 2 minutes. Don't mix for too long or the cookies might bake flat. Add the egg and vanilla and beat for another minute, or until thoroughly combined.

With the mixer running on low speed, add the flour mixture all at once and mix until thoroughly blended, scraping down the sides of the bowl once or twice.

In a separate bowl, toss together the pecans and chocolate chunks. Add them to the cookie dough in a steady stream and mix just to combine.

Divide the dough into ¼-cup-size balls and set them roughly 2 inches apart on a pair of ungreased baking sheets. Flatten the balls slightly with the palm of your hand. Refrigerate the baking sheets for 15 minutes. (This helps prevent a flat cookie.)

Bake for 15 to 20 minutes, until the cookies just start to turn golden brown. They should still be a little soft in the center.

These cookies are best eaten the day they are made, but will keep in an airtight container at room temperature for up to 3 days.

CHOCOLATE OATMEAL ALE COOKIES
with CARAMEL ICING

SOFIA VARANKA HUDSON, Swoon
Kansas City, Missouri

A little bit of dark beer is like a handsome stranger, adding the right touch of intrigue to a cookie. Here, the strong ale lends a toffeelike quality to the caramel. A bit sticky and a bit chewy, these ale cookies show off more depth with each bite.

This is liquid heaven for chocoholics. On some top secret delicious mission, the cocoa in the cookies seeks out the chocolate malt in the beer for a lovely choco-centric finish. The beer responds in kind by rounding out those toffee notes in the caramel.

MAKES: 24 cookies
PAIRING: New Belgium Brewing Company's 1554 Black Lager
STYLE: Black lagers have hints of coffee and chocolate without a bitter finish. The beer has enough body to match up with the caramel, but isn't so busy that the cookie gets lost.

1 (12-ounce) bottle Belgian strong dark ale

2½ cups old-fashioned rolled oats

2½ cups all-purpose flour

⅓ cup unsweetened Dutch-process cocoa powder

1½ teaspoons baking powder

1½ teaspoons baking soda

1 teaspoon ground cinnamon

½ teaspoon salt

1 cup (2 sticks) salted butter, at room temperature

1 cup granulated sugar

1 cup firmly packed dark brown sugar

2 large eggs, at room temperature

10 ounces caramel candies (such as Brach's)

Pour ⅓ cup of the ale into a glass and stir until the carbonation is removed. Set aside. Pour the rest of the bottle into a small saucepan and set aside.

Preheat the oven to 350°F. Line two baking sheets with parchment paper or lightly butter them.

In a blender or food processor, pulverize the oats until they have the consistency of bread crumbs. Add the flour, cocoa, baking powder, baking soda, cinnamon, and salt. Pulse until blended. Set aside.

In the bowl of a stand mixer fitted with the paddle attachment, beat the butter on low speed until creamy, 2 to 3 minutes. Slowly add the granulated sugar and brown sugar. Mix on low speed until light and creamy. Add the eggs, one at a time, and then the ⅓ cup of flat ale. Mix until uniform in color, then slowly add the oat mixture until completely incorporated.

Scoop heaping tablespoons of the dough and place them at least 2 inches apart on the baking sheets. Refrigerate the baking sheets for at least 15 minutes.

Meanwhile, heat the saucepan with the ale over medium-low heat until the beer has reduced to ¼ cup. Add the caramels to the reduced ale and stir until melted. Remove from the heat but keep warm.

Before putting the baking sheets in the oven, flatten the cookies slightly with a fork or your palm. Bake for 7 minutes, then rotate the baking sheets 180 degrees and bake for 8 minutes more. The cookies are done when they bounce back if lightly pressed.

Transfer the cookies to a wire rack set over a baking sheet and let cool. Once they're cool to the touch, drizzle the cookies with the caramel. Allow the caramel to set up.

These cookies are best eaten the day they're baked.

CHEF AMY'S CHOCOLATE CHIP COOKIES

AMY LEMON, pastry chef, Emeril's Delmonico Restaurant
New Orleans, Louisiana

The browned butter in this recipe is the reason these chocolate chip cookies are special. It makes them taste like caramel and lets the chocolate hover on your tongue. The salt on top hypes up the vanilla and plays off that caramel character.

The sweetness and creaminess of the milk stout wraps around the cookie—it's all the comfort of milk in a beer. The cookie, in turn, brings out the latent chocolate notes of the beer. Start with two of each, even if you're eating by yourself.

MAKES: 24 cookies
PAIRING: Left Hand Brewing Company's Milk Stout
STYLE: Milk stouts are sweet and creamy. With the right chocolate chip cookie, they're the missing link between milk and beer.

2¼ cups bread flour

1 teaspoon baking soda

¾ teaspoon salt

1 cup (2 sticks) unsalted butter

1 vanilla bean, halved lengthwise and seeds scraped

1 cup firmly packed light brown sugar plus 2 tablespoons

¼ cup granulated sugar

1 large egg

1 large egg yolk

1 ounce 2% milk (skim milk will work, too)

6 ounces milk chocolate candy bar, chopped into ½-inch chunks

6 ounces dark chocolate candy bar, chopped into ½-inch chunks

Vanilla fleur de sel, for sprinkling (see Note)

NOTE: Split a vanilla bean lengthwise and scrape out the seeds into a small bowl. In a separate mixing bowl, combine ¼ cup sea salt and the vanilla seeds. Mix the salt and seeds gently together with your hands. Use a small, resealable glass jar for the mixture and store in a cool, dry place.

In a medium bowl, combine the flour, baking soda, and salt. Set aside.

Heat a medium saucepan over medium heat. Add the butter and let it melt, then cook, swirling occasionally, until the milk solids turn golden brown and the butter foams and begins to smell nutty. Remove from the heat and add the vanilla bean pod and seeds. Set aside until cooled to room temperature, then remove the vanilla bean pod and save it for another use.

CONTINUED ON PAGE 32

CHEF AMY'S CHOCOLATE CHIP COOKIES

CONTINUED

Pour the cooled brown butter into the bowl of a stand mixer fitted with the paddle attachment. Add the brown sugar and granulated sugar and cream together on low speed until pale and fluffy.

Add the egg, then the egg yolk and mix, scraping down the sides of the bowl as necessary.

Turn off the mixer and add the flour mixture. Mix on very low speed just until the dough begins to come together. Drizzle in the milk, then add the chocolate and mix just until the dough comes together. Wrap the dough in plastic wrap and refrigerate for at least 1 hour.

Position a rack in the center of the oven and preheat the oven to 350°F. Line two baking sheets with parchment paper.

Scoop 2-ounce portions of the dough and roll them between your hands to form smooth balls. Set the dough balls at least 3 inches apart on the prepared baking sheets. Bake for 7 minutes, then remove from the oven and sprinkle the top of each cookie lightly with fleur de sel. Return the cookies to the oven and bake until they are lightly golden around the edges but still soft to the touch, 5 to 6 minutes more. Remove from the oven and place the baking sheets on wire racks to cool briefly before transferring the cookies to the racks. Serve the cookies warm, but they will keep in an airtight container at room temperature for 2 to 3 days.

CHOCOLATE-ALMOND-COCONUT MACAROONS

STEVEN SATTERFIELD, Miller Union
Atlanta, Georgia

The chocolate, almond, and coconut all work together to create this well-balanced cookie that has a righteous chew and just enough crust to bring it home.

The simplicity of the cookie plays off the complexity of The Reverend. You'll taste some dark fruit in this big beer, which has a touch of sweetness and an easy finish. This is the dark chocolate–dipped cherry that the world needs.

MAKES: 96 small or 48 large cookies
PAIRING: Avery Brewing Company's The Reverend
STYLE: You can reach for a quadrupel (quad) or a Belgian strong ale to give you a big, dark brew with some underlying spiciness.

1 cup blanched almonds

6 large egg whites

½ teaspoon fine sea salt

2 cups sugar

½ teaspoon vanilla extract

12 ounces 70% cacao dark chocolate, melted

1 cup unsweetened grated coconut

Chop the almonds roughly on a cutting board with a non-serrated knife. In a food processor, pulse the almonds in small, short bursts until the nuts are evenly ground into a fine meal that looks like coarse sand. Set aside. In the bowl of a stand mixer fitted with the whisk attachment, or in a clean bowl using a whisk or a hand mixer, beat the egg whites and salt until stiff but not dry. Beat in the sugar, a little at a time. The mixture should be thick and glossy and stand in peaks. Using a spatula, gently fold in the almonds, vanilla, and melted chocolate. Cover and refrigerate the dough overnight.

Preheat the oven to 350°F. Line two baking sheets with parchment paper.

Spread the coconut in a shallow dish. Drop 1 teaspoon (or 2 teaspoons, for large cookies) of the dough into the coconut and roll to coat. Place the coconut-coated dough balls at least 1 inch apart on the prepared baking sheets. Bake for 12 to 15 minutes, until the tops are lightly firm to the touch. Let cool.

The cookies will keep in an airtight container at room temperature for up to 1 week.

CHOCOLATE-COVERED CARAMEL-FILLED SHORTBREAD COOKIES

J. KENJI LOPÉZ-ALT, *Serious Eats*

You didn't know that a Twix needed to be fixed, but then this cookie shows up in your life. The shortbread cookie adds a great crumble, while the caramel has a deep buttery richness. These dark chocolate–dipped discs are Halloween in reverse. You won't want to share them with the kids.

The Black Butte Porter feels like a beer designed for candy. It's got a secret vein of chocolate and a creaminess that amplifies the caramel in the cookie. The light body has a biscuitlike quality that mirrors the shortbread, and the brew has just a touch of bitterness to tone down the cookies.

MAKES: 24 cookies
PAIRING: Deschutes Brewery's Black Butte Porter
STYLE: A porter or barrel-aged porter will play nicely with the shortbread, caramel, and chocolate.

SHORTBREAD COOKIES

½ cup steel-cut oats

1½ cups all-purpose flour

¼ cup cornstarch

⅔ cup confectioners' sugar

½ teaspoon salt

14 tablespoons (1¾ sticks) unsalted butter, cut into tablespoon-size pats

CARAMEL FILLING

¾ cup sweetened condensed milk

6 tablespoons (¾ stick) unsalted butter

½ cup granulated sugar

½ cup firmly packed dark brown sugar

½ cup corn syrup

¼ teaspoon salt

½ teaspoon vanilla extract

To make the shortbread cookies, preheat the oven to 350°F. Line a baking sheet with parchment paper.

In a food processor or blender, grind the oats into a fine flour and transfer to the bowl of a stand mixer fitted with the paddle attachment. Add the flour, cornstarch, confectioners' sugar, and salt. Mix on low speed until combined, about 15 seconds. Add the butter and beat on low speed until a dough forms and pulls away from the sides of the bowl, about 12 minutes.

Place a sheet of parchment paper on your work surface and turn out the dough onto the parchment paper. Form the dough into a ball and flatten it slightly. Lay a second sheet of parchment paper on top and roll with a rolling pin into an even layer about ¼ inch thick. Remove the top sheet of parchment paper and cut out circles of the dough using a 2½-inch round cookie cutter. Place half of those circles on the prepared baking sheet.

CONTINUED ▸→

CHOCOLATE-COVERED CARAMEL-FILLED SHORTBREAD COOKIES

CONTINUED

CHOCOLATE COATING

20 ounces (3⅓ cups) bittersweet chocolate discs, chips, or coarsely smashed bars

Coarse sea salt (such as Maldon)

Use a 2¼-inch cookie cutter to cut a second circle out of the center of the remaining circles. Top each of the circles on the baking sheet with one of the punched-out rings of dough, pressing down slightly to adhere them together. Prick the center of each cookie four times (it'll look like a giant button) with a wooden toothpick to dock.

Gather up the dough scraps and repeat the rolling, cutting, and topping.

Bake the cookies for 10 to 12 minutes, until the edges are lightly golden brown. Let them cool completely on a wire rack with waxed or parchment paper underneath (you'll need it to catch dripping chocolate later).

To make the caramel, in a medium saucepan, combine the condensed milk, butter, granulated sugar, dark brown sugar, corn syrup, salt, ¼ cup water, and vanilla. Bring to a boil over medium high heat, stirring continuously with a rubber spatula. When the mixture reaches 245°F on an instant-read thermometer, immediately remove it from the heat and pour it into a 2-cup liquid measure.

Spoon the caramel into the center of each cookie, until it is just above the lip of the shortbread ring on top. Let cool.

While the caramel is cooling, you can make the chocolate coating. Set aside one-quarter of the chocolate. Place the rest in a microwave-safe bowl and microwave it in 15-second intervals, stirring after each interval, until the temperature registers 115°F. Add half of the chocolate you set aside to the heated chocolate in the bowl. Stir vigorously with a rubber spatula. Add the remaining portion of the unmelted chocolate while stirring until the temperature measures 85°F. Place the bowl in the microwave for 10-second intervals, stirring between intervals, until the chocolate registers 90°F.

Pour or spoon the melted chocolate over the cookies, letting the excess drip through the wire rack. Let the chocolate cool for 1 minute and then sprinkle coarse sea salt on the center. Let the chocolate harden for 10 minutes more on the counter, then refrigerate for 10 minutes before serving.

The cookies will keep in an airtight container at room temperature for up to 5 days.

TIP: Any leftover caramel can be poured into a lightly buttered baking dish. Once it has cooled to room temperature, you can cut it into individual caramel candies.

VALRHONA CHOCOLATE CHIP COOKIES

WILLIAM WERNER, chef/partner, Craftsman and Wolves
San Francisco, California

The salt in this cookie is brilliant, a Trojan horse designed to turn savory fans into sweets lovers. The salty first bite opens the door for the dark chocolate, and the two find each other in the chewy center thanks to the recipe's use of bread flour.

This dark brew holds a bourbon-tinged storm inside that is unlocked by dark chocolate. After the first sip of beer, the lingering salt will keep you sipping the Old Viscosity and enjoying its great caramel finish.

MAKES: 15 cookies
PAIRING: Port Brewing Company's Old Viscosity Ale
STYLE: Look for the words "dark strong ale," "imperial porter," or "imperial stout"—you want a big, dark brew aged in bourbon barrels to highlight the salt and match the rich, dark chocolate.

2 cups plus 2 tablespoons all-purpose flour

1¼ cups high-gluten bread flour

¾ teaspoon baking soda

1½ teaspoons baking powder

1¼ teaspoons salt

⅓ cup plus 1 tablespoon granulated sugar

1 cup firmly packed dark brown sugar

1 vanilla bean, halved lengthwise and seeds scraped

1 cup (2 sticks) unsalted butter, at room temperature

2 large eggs, at room temperature

2 cups chopped 80% cacao Valrhona chocolate

Maldon sea salt, for sprinkling

In a large bowl, whisk together the all-purpose flour, bread flour, baking soda, baking powder, and salt, then sift through a fine-mesh sieve. Set aside. In a small bowl, combine the granulated sugar, brown sugar, and vanilla bean seeds until mixed evenly.

In the bowl of a stand mixer fitted with the paddle attachment, cream together the butter and sugar mixture on medium-low speed until the mixture is even and there are no visible chunks of butter. (Take care not to overmix or the cookies will spread out too much during baking.)

Scrape down the bowl. With the mixer running on medium-low speed, add the eggs one at a time, waiting until the first is fully incorporated before adding the next. With the mixer on the lowest speed, add the dry ingredients in three batches. Right before the last addition is fully incorporated, add the chopped chocolate. Mix until the dough is even and there is no visible flour. Cover the bowl with plastic wrap and let the dough rest in the refrigerator overnight.

Preheat the oven to 350°F. Line a baking sheet with parchment paper.

Scoop ⅓-cup portions of the dough and evenly space six portions on the prepared baking sheet. Sprinkle a small amount of sea salt on the tops of the cookies. Bake for 20 to 25 minutes, until the edges are set, the middle is slightly puffed, and each cookie is a nice even brown color. Let the cookies set for 5 minutes, then transfer to a wire rack to cool. Repeat with the remaining dough until all the cookies are baked.

The cookies will keep in an airtight container at room temperature for 3 to 5 days.

GIRL SCOUT COOKIES & BEER

I grew up with a family that didn't believe in delaying satisfaction when it came to food. There was, however, a singular notable exception to the rules of the dinner table: Thin Mints.

Each spring, my father would purchase boxes of the crisp, dark chocolate–enrobed mint cookies, like a squirrel given an open line of credit at the nut store. A few more of the green boxes would appear each day, stacked in the pantry and freezer (a frozen Thin Mint lasts longer and has a particular snap that fans will know) with the implicit understanding that no hands other than my dad's should tear into the two matching silver foil tubes inside.

We knew that the cookies had to last the year. They never did. But a few years, we nearly made it to summer. The return of Girl Scout Cookies each spring is a celebration. And now that I've become a father myself, I understand the joy of doling out cookies or sneaking a couple on the car ride home. In order to guide your celebration, here are a few Girl Scout Cookies and beer pairings that you shouldn't wait to try.

LEMONADES & BELGIAN IPA—The tangy lemon-iced shortbread has this big burst of sweetness that is properly corralled by the hops in a Belgian IPA. The citrus in the cookie will bring out the same in the beer for a zesty combination that is sweet and bright, like adult candy.

CARAMEL DELITES (SAMOAS) & SCOTCH ALES—This is the cardigan sweater of beer and cookie pairings. Warm, comforting, and exactly what you want to wrap yourself in while you lay around on the couch. Scotch ale, also known as "Wee Heavy," has caramel undertones and maltiness that go well with the caramel and toasted coconut in the Samoas.

SHORTBREAD (TREFOILS) & OYSTER STOUT—Fit for the Great Gatsby himself, this pairing pits the flaky, buttery shortbread with rich, toasty stout. Just as this brew was once enjoyed with oysters on the half shell, the common toffee or caramel notes will play well with the butter and vanilla in the shortbread.

PEANUT BUTTER PATTIES (TAGALONGS) & BROWN ALE—This is about inventing another classic. Peanut butter and chocolate are best friends—hence the winning combination of a crunchy cookie center enrobed in peanut butter and chocolate. But both could find a new nutty friend with hints of chocolate in the brown ale. The brew mellows out the cookie.

THIN MINTS & IMPERIAL STOUT—Mint is tricky. And it's understandable to not want to mess with the peppermint oil–infused dark chocolate cookies. But imperial stout has these big coffee notes that turn this combo into an adult take on a peppermint mocha.

FRUIT

ORANGE & GINGER
SPICED COOKIES • 43

PUMPKIN CHOCOLATE
CHIP COOKIES • 46

PEACH AND HEFEWEIZEN JAM
BROWN BUTTER THUMBPRINT
COOKIES • 48

MAPLE FIG
SHORTBREAD COOKIES • 50

PUMPKIN BUTTERSCOTCH
COOKIES • 52

ALMOND APRICOT
WHITE CHOCOLATE CHUNK
COOKIES • 54

"I love the way your teeth break the **CRUNCHY SURFACE** of a cookie to reveal an *inner chewy* layer that **BREAKS** into crumbs on your tongue and then dissolves into a *soul-satisfying* swallow."

ANNE CROY, pastry chef, Pastaria

Fruit in beer and fruit with beer are easy targets for beer snobs and comedians alike. The suggestion is that fruit is not manly or relevant to beer. The reality is that while some guys are busy puffing out their chests, the rest of us are happily filling our bellies. Here, we rebuild fruit and beer's image with combinations, like the ALMOND APRICOT WHITE CHOCOLATE CHUNK COOKIES (page 54) and AVERY BREWING COMPANY'S ELLIE'S BROWN ALE, that are complex and comforting at the same time. These cookies also highlight ingredients like pumpkin and apricot that could use champions in their own right.

Fruit cookies for me will forever be entwined with a spring carnival—the kind where you win a fish by throwing a Ping-Pong ball into a fish bowl. The spring carnival stands out, because it introduced me to my first great fruit cookie. An apricot hamantasch—a traditional Jewish pastry for the spring holiday of Purim—had a simple sweetness from the bright orange jam that rested inside a lemon zest–spiked triangular cookie. It was light and gone all too soon—just like the fish that accompanied us home.

ORANGE & GINGER
SPICED COOKIES

CHRISTOPHER ELBOW ARTISANAL CHOCOLATE
Kansas City, Missouri

Thin and really crispy, these cookies put the snap back in gingersnap. They have the bright spice of ginger without being overwhelming thanks to the radiant undercurrent of orange. These, like great potato chips, are all about the crunch.

Boulevard's 80 Acre resets your palate with each sip. The hops meld with the ginger and find the citrus. After that, the wheat brew and orange live happily ever after.

MAKES: 24 cookies

PAIRING: Boulevard Brewing Company's 80-Acre Hoppy Wheat

STYLE: Hoppy wheats are a bit like unicorns. If you can't track one down, opt for a porter. The medium-bodied brew accentuates the orange and ginger.

2½ cups all-purpose flour, plus more for dusting

½ teaspoon baking soda

¼ teaspoon salt

2 teaspoons ground ginger

2 teaspoons ground cinnamon

½ teaspoon ground cloves

½ cup (1 stick) unsalted butter, at room temperature

½ cup sugar

1 tablespoon finely grated orange zest

1 large egg

½ cup molasses

In a large bowl, sift together the flour, baking soda, salt, ginger, cinnamon, and cloves.

In the bowl of a stand mixer fitted with the paddle attachment, cream together the butter, sugar, and orange zest until fluffy. Add the egg and mix until incorporated. Add the molasses and mix until incorporated. Gradually add the flour mixture in three batches and mix until just combined. Flatten the dough into a disc and wrap it in plastic wrap. Refrigerate for 2 hours or overnight.

Preheat the oven to 350°F. Line a baking sheet with a silicone baking mat.

CONTINUED ⇢→

ORANGE & GINGER
SPICED COOKIES

Lightly flour your work surface. While the dough is still cold, roll it out to ⅛ inch thick. Cut out cookies with a 2½ or 3-inch round or fluted-edge cookie cutter and place them ½ inch apart on the prepared baking sheet. Bake for 8 to 10 minutes, until slightly browned around the edges. Let cool completely.

The cookies will keep in an airtight container at room temperature for 3 to 5 days.

PUMPKIN
CHOCOLATE CHIP COOKIES

STACY BEGIN, Two Fat Cats Bakery
Portland, Maine

The pumpkin spice invasion has made us forget what was great about pumpkin in the first place: a subtle earthy flavor that speaks to fall and Halloween. These homey, chewy, pumpkin cookies keep the shape of however you drop them on the baking sheet, so they're almost like mini muffin tops with crispy edges. The cinnamon and vanilla come through, but only after the chocolate and pumpkin have a chance to meet your taste buds. Sometimes, you need a little spice with your pumpkin.

When you add Old Rasputin Imperial Stout to the pumpkin chocolate chip cookie, it's like you've just invented creamy pumpkin pie without the pie. The cookie pops up to lend lushness to this big, dark beer.

MAKES: 24 cookies
PAIRING: North Coast Brewing Co. Old Rasputin Imperial Stout
STYLE: You want an imperial stout, sometimes known as a Russian imperial stout—a big brew with high alcohol by volume content that goes well with pumpkin cookies, as well as pumpkin pie.

Butter, for the baking sheet
4 cups all-purpose flour
2 teaspoons baking powder
2 teaspoons ground cinnamon
1 teaspoon salt
2 teaspoons milk (whatever you have on hand)
2 teaspoons baking soda
2 medium eggs
1 (15-ounce) can pumpkin purée
1 cup vegetable oil
2 teaspoons vanilla extract
2 cups sugar
1 (12-ounce) bag semisweet chocolate chips

Preheat the oven to 375°F. Grease a baking sheet with butter.

In a large bowl, combine the flour, baking powder, cinnamon, and salt. Mix with a wooden spoon until the color is uniform. Set aside.

In a large bowl, whisk together the milk and baking soda until the baking soda has dissolved and there are no lumps, about 2 minutes.

Crack the eggs into a small bowl and beat lightly with a fork until the yolks and whites are combined. Add the eggs, pumpkin, oil, vanilla, and sugar to the bowl with the milk and baking soda. Mix well with a whisk until the color and consistency are uniform.

Add the flour mixture and use a wooden spoon to mix until the flour mixture is almost fully incorporated. Consider sitting with the bowl in your lap—you'll need some arm strength over the 3 minutes or so you're stirring.

Add the chocolate chips, stirring only until the chips are distributed throughout the batter.

Drop heaping teaspoons of the batter 1½ to 2 inches apart on the prepared baking sheet. Bake for 12 to 15 minutes. The cookies are done when they puff up and the tops feel firm to the touch. Let them cool for about 5 minutes before transferring them to a wire rack.

The cookies will keep in an airtight container at room temperature for 3 to 5 days.

PEACH AND HEFEWEIZEN JAM
BROWN BUTTER THUMBPRINT
C O O K I E S

MANDY PUNTNEY, 4&20 Bakery and Café
Madison, Wisconsin

These cookies have a lovely lightness, and they capture that great forbidden moment in an orchard when you bite into a piece of fruit you've just picked instead of placing it in your basket. (Added bonus: There's no juice on your shirt as evidence.) The jam has a burst of dazzling peach nestled into the rich, nutty cookie.

The Island Wheat ale brings the citrus forward in the cookies, which in turn unlocks a bit of honey in the brew. The straw-colored beer smells of wheat, and that tiny bit of earthiness warms the almond and peaches. The beer has a delicate, slightly dry finish that also tempers the cookie's sweetness.

MAKES: 24 cookies
PAIRING: Capital Brewery's Island Wheat
STYLE: An American pale wheat ale will be light and bright, a great complement to the Hefeweizen in the cookie.

JAM

1½ pounds fresh peaches (frozen will work, too)

6 ounces Capital Brewery's Island Wheat (or any available wheat beer)

Finely grated zest and juice of 1 large orange

1 tablespoon fresh lemon juice

3 tablespoons pectin (such as Sure-Jell)

¾ cup granulated sugar

To make the jam, wash, peel, pit, and slice the peaches. Purée the sliced peaches in a blender or food processor.

Transfer the peach purée to a large heavy-bottomed saucepan and add the beer, orange zest, orange juice, lemon juice, and pectin. Bring the mixture to a boil over medium-high heat. Add the sugar and cook, stirring frequently, for 15 minutes. Remove the pan from the heat and let cool. Transfer to a bowl or covered container and refrigerate overnight.

To make the cookies, in a medium saucepan, melt the butter over medium heat, stirring frequently as the milk solids brown. When the milk solids sink to the bottom, take the pan off the heat and pour the butter into a heatproof container. Set aside to cool to room temperature.

Preheat the oven to 350°F. Line a baking sheet with parchment paper.

In the bowl of a stand mixer fitted with the paddle attachment, cream together the cooled browned butter, granulated sugar, vanilla, and almond extract until pale and fluffy. Chop the almonds roughly on a cutting board with a non-serrated knife. In a food processor, pulse the almonds in small, short bursts until the nuts are evenly ground into a fine meal that looks like coarse sand. Add the ground almonds and flour to the mixing bowl and mix until incorporated.

Roll the dough into 1-inch balls and place them 2 inches apart on the prepared baking sheet. Take your index finger or the handle of a wooden spoon and make an indentation in the center of each dough ball.

Bake for 15 to 18 minutes, until the edges begin to brown. Remove the cookies from the oven and make the indentation deeper with the spoon handle. Be careful not to go all the way through the cookie. Let cool completely. Sprinkle with confectioners' sugar and use a small spoon to fill the indentation with some of the jam. Give them 1 hour for the jam to set before eating.

These cookies will keep in an airtight container at room temperature for 5 days.

COOKIES

1 cup (2 sticks) plus
2 tablespoons unsalted butter

½ cup granulated sugar

1 teaspoon vanilla extract

½ teaspoon almond extract

1¾ cups ground blanched almonds

1¾ cups all-purpose flour

Confectioners' sugar, for dusting

MAPLE FIG SHORTBREAD COOKIES

FORREST WRIGHT, PT's Coffee
Topeka, Kansas

These cookies score high on the low-effort, maximum-deliciousness scale. The figs shine with the sugar and maple syrup, bringing out the honeylike sweetness of the fruit. This cookie has a crumbly exterior and pillowy interior, the dessert cousin of a perfectly cooked french fry.

Boulevard's Saison-Brett funks things up. The funky earth notes from the yeast strain used for the beer are great partners to the maple and fig sweetness in the cookie. You'll taste echoes of the fig in the saison, and the slightly dry finish is spot-on.

MAKES: 24 cookies
PAIRING: Boulevard Brewing Company's Saison-Brett
STYLE: A saison or a Belgian strong dark ale will help match and tame the richness of the butter, maple, and fig.

2 cups all-purpose flour

½ cup confectioners' sugar

Pinch of salt

1 cup (2 sticks) unsalted butter, at room temperature

1 teaspoon vanilla extract

3 tablespoons dark amber maple syrup

1 cup dried black Mission figs, stemmed and halved

In a large bowl, combine the flour, sugar, and salt. Stir with a spatula until combined. Add the butter and stir until the dough is evenly coated and moist. Add the vanilla and maple syrup and mix until combined, about 1 minute. Add the figs and mix until they are distributed throughout the dough.

Place plastic wrap on a flat surface. Turn out the dough onto the plastic wrap and roll it into a cylinder shape, about 10 inches in length. Wrap the dough cylinder in plastic wrap and refrigerate for 15 minutes, or until firm to the touch.

Preheat the oven to 350°F. Line a baking sheet with parchment paper.

Slice the dough into ½-inch-thick discs and place them about ½ inch apart on the prepared baking sheet. Bake for 10 to 12 minutes, until the edges of the cookies are light brown.

The cookies will keep in an airtight container at room temperature for 2 to 4 days.

PUMPKIN BUTTERSCOTCH COOKIES

KATE & SCOTT MEINKE, Heirloom Bakery & Hearth
Kansas City, Missouri

As the weather gets cooler, pumpkin pie and its gang of warming spices (I see you, nutmeg) always sound appealing. Here, it's like rogue diner elves have snuck in and wisely decided to top pumpkin pie with butterscotch whipped cream. This rounded, soft-centered cookie is a sweet fall crush.

A bit boozy, the Bourbon Barrel Quad makes you feel warm. In the midst of those good feelings, it's also got caramel and vanilla undertones thanks to the time it spends aging in oak barrels. The cookie and brew together are as comforting as cocoa and marshmallows.

MAKES: about 18 cookies
PAIRING: Boulevard Brewing Company's Bourbon Barrel Quad
STYLE: A bourbon barrel–aged brew will give you a big warming effect, while a Hefeweizen is a lighter alternative with complementary butterscotch notes.

3 cups all-purpose flour

½ teaspoon baking powder

½ teaspoon baking soda

½ teaspoon coarse kosher salt

½ teaspoon freshly grated nutmeg

½ teaspoon ground allspice

½ teaspoon ground ginger

1 cup (2 sticks) unsalted butter, at room temperature

½ cup granulated sugar

2 cups firmly packed light brown sugar

2 teaspoons vanilla extract

¾ cup pumpkin purée

1 cup finely chopped pecans

1 cup butterscotch chips

Preheat the oven to 350°F. Line a baking sheet with parchment paper.

In a medium bowl, combine the flour, baking powder, baking soda, salt, nutmeg, allspice, and ginger. Set aside.

In the bowl of a stand mixer fitted with the paddle attachment, cream the butter on medium speed for about 30 seconds. Add the granulated sugar and brown sugar and mix on medium speed until fluffy. Add the vanilla and pumpkin purée and mix until well combined, scraping down the sides of bowl with spatula, if needed.

Gradually add the flour mixture to the pumpkin mixture and mix until well combined. Add the pecans and butterscotch chips and mix until fully incorporated into the dough. The dough can be covered and refrigerated for up to 4 days.

Use a ⅓-cup measuring scoop or ice cream scoop to form balls and place about 1½ inches apart on the prepared baking sheet. Press down gently with your palm to slightly flatten the cookies. Bake for 13 to 15 minutes, rotating the baking sheet 180 degrees halfway through, until the edges begin to firm but the center is still soft. Let the cookies cool on the baking sheet for 7 minutes before transferring them to a wire rack.

The cookies will keep in an airtight container at room temperature for 7 to 10 days.

NOTE: To make your own pumpkin purée, find a small pumpkin (not the type you'd carve for a jack-o'-lantern) at a farmers' market or grocery store. Cut the pumpkin in half from top to bottom and scoop out the seeds. Place both halves on a baking sheet, cut-side down. Poke the outer skin all over with a fork. Bake at 375°F for 50 minutes, or until the pumpkin is tender and soft when poked with a fork. Let cool. Scoop out the insides and purée in a blender or food processor until smooth. The purée can be stored in an airtight container in the fridge for up to 7 days.

ALMOND APRICOT WHITE CHOCOLATE CHUNK COOKIES

NATASHA GOELLNER, Natasha's Mulberry & Mott
Kansas City, Missouri

This cookie's chew is otherworldly. The crust melts into the munchy interior where sweet little pockets of apricot and white chocolate await. A ribbon of almond flavor runs through the whole cookie, connecting each of the parts to produce a dessert that's sublime.

Ellie's Brown Ale has echoes of vanilla, nuts, and brown sugar. Those subtle notes match the cookie, helping the apricot and white chocolate ride on your tongue like a wave that makes it all the way to the beach.

MAKES: 15 cookies
PAIRING: Avery Brewing Company's Ellie's Brown Ale
STYLE: A brown ale will make you want to dunk this cookie because it lets the sweetness linger and is as comforting and smooth as milk.

½ cup (1 stick) unsalted butter, at room temperature

1 cup granulated sugar

1 cup firmly packed light brown sugar

½ cup almond paste

2 tablespoons vanilla extract

2 large eggs

3½ cups all-purpose flour

1 teaspoon kosher salt

2 teaspoons baking soda

1 cup white chocolate chips

1 cup coarsely chopped dried apricots

Preheat the oven to 350°F. Line a baking sheet with parchment paper.

In the bowl of a stand mixer fitted with the paddle attachment, cream together the butter, granulated sugar, brown sugar, almond paste, and vanilla on medium speed until smooth. Add the eggs one at a time, scraping down the bowl and paddle after each addition. Once the eggs are well incorporated, add the flour, salt, baking soda, white chocolate, and apricots. Mix on low speed until combined. The dough shouldn't be too sticky.

Use a 4-ounce ice cream scoop (or ½-cup measuring cup) to scoop portions of the dough and place them about 2 inches apart on the prepared baking sheet. Lightly flatten the cookies with your palm. Bake for 14 minutes, or until golden brown around the sides and still pale in the center. Let cool on the baking sheet for 5 minutes before transferring to a wire rack.

The cookies will keep in an airtight container at room temperature for 2 days.

BEER MILK SHAKES

Beer milk shakes are all too often like the toy surprise in your cereal—full of promise and enticing names, but arriving on your table accompanied by disappointment. They can be lumpy affairs, alternating between sips of chalky booze and cloying ice cream.

As a result, the beer milk shake has been labeled a novelty drink—the thing you choke down while silently telling yourself you won't make the same mis-shake twice. I still shudder to think of a pint glass in Brooklyn that smelled like the floor of a college bar in the early mornings and tasted like the mop that had just gone over said floor. But we haven't given the beer milk shake a fair shake. We've been going at it all wrong.

The prevailing wisdom is that you just throw some beer in a blender with ice cream and syrup. This approach can yield tasty results through happy accidents or fond recollections—end-of-the-night drinks often have better reputations than they deserve. But the blend-it-if-you-got-it technique is more likely to bring out the things in beer that you don't like—bitterness or booziness, strong characteristics that take away from the consistent richness that is a hallmark of a great shake. You want to be lulled into a comfortable state of sipping that leaves you

sitting demonstrably lower in the booth over the course of your meal—not clucking your tongue on the bottom of your mouth like a cat in the middle of a cleaning.

Mixing beer and ice cream can be delicious. Guinness—the Irish stout that makes its way into cupcakes and brownies around St. Patrick's Day—is made for a heaping scoop of vanilla ice cream. The sweetness of the vanilla (plus a touch of nutmeg, added in the same fashion that you might spice chili or oatmeal) finds a willing partner in the creamy stout. It's that spirit we want to emulate with beer milk shakes.

The answer to this cool conundrum is a little bit of heat. The following page has a recipe for beer syrup, basically a beer reduction with a heaping shot of sugar. The syrup you'll be producing helps distill the beer flavor without amplifying the harsher notes. The syrup can be used in cocktails, drizzled over sundaes, and, most important, used as the foundation for a good milk shake.

BEER SYRUP

MAKES ABOUT 4 OUNCES

12 ounces dark beer
(stout or porter)

½ cup turbinado sugar
(such as Sugar in the Raw)

In a large nonstick saucepan, bring the beer to a boil over medium heat, stirring gently. As soon as the beer boils, reduce the heat to medium-low. The beer needs to be simmering with small bubbles on the surface, but not frothy. Simmer for 35 to 45 minutes, stirring every 3 or 4 minutes to make sure it doesn't burn. The beer will begin to thicken as it reduces and may get slightly darker in color. After 30 minutes, stir every 2 to 3 minutes to keep the reduction from sticking to the bottom of the pot.

Remove the pan from the heat and pour the beer into a heat-resistant bowl. Add the sugar to the bowl. Stir with a whisk until the sugar has completely dissolved. Let cool completely, about 90 minutes.

The syrup will keep in an airtight container in the refrigerator for about 2 weeks.

BEER MILK SHAKE

The beer syrup adds a caramel-y hint to a classic version of a black and white milk shake. Thick, rich, and satisfying, this shake is a winner of a dessert.

MAKES 1 MILK SHAKE

2 cups vanilla ice cream

½ cup whole milk

2 ounces chocolate syrup

2 ounces Beer Syrup

In a blender, combine the ice cream, milk, chocolate syrup, and beer syrup and blend on medium speed until smooth.

NOTE: This is a base recipe that you can adjust with different flavors of ice cream and ratios of chocolate (or other flavors) to beer syrup. You can combine vanilla (or butter pecan) ice cream with salted caramel syrup (sometimes called caramel topping) to make a slamming caramel shake, peanut butter ice cream with chocolate syrup for a classic peanut butter chocolate shake, or mint chocolate chip with hot fudge topping for a luscious mint chocolate shake. Just keep the four-to-one ratio of ice cream to milk the same, and the rest will work just fine.

SAVORY

RICH BUTTER COOKIES
WITH FENNEL SEED
AND SEA SALT • 61

OLIVE OIL AND ALMOND
BISCOTTI • 64

CURRY COCONUT
MACAROONS • 66

CHAI SPICE • 68

BATCH BAKEHOUSE'S
VANILLA BASIL SHORTIE • 70

"You can eat *cookies* while **RIDING** a bike. You can make them into a **SANDWICH**. You can have one in one hand and a *beer* in the other hand!"

MOLLY YEH, *My Name Is Yeh*

A touch of salt. The smell of fennel. Savory elements in cookies are like *The Baby-Sitters Club* for beers: They uncover hidden mysteries in ways that are incredibly easy to follow and perfectly palatable, and make you anxious to start the next one after you finish.

Since we're confessing to guilty pleasures (gosh, Dawn and Mary Anne could solve anything), I eat soft-baked pretzels everywhere: movie theaters, ballparks, gas stations. It's my secret vice and greatest eternal disappointment. I want that bit of bready sweetness and a big punch of salt. The spice rack's worth of cookies in this chapter, like the RICH BUTTER COOKIES WITH FENNEL SEED AND SEA SALT (page 61) with LAGUNITAS BREWING COMPANY'S CENSORED RICH COPPER ALE, offer me hope. If I can fit an Easy-Bake Oven in my glovebox, I think I've got the cure right here.

RICH BUTTER COOKIES *with* FENNEL SEED AND SEA SALT

AMY BEEMAN, South End Buttery
Boston, Massachusetts

You'll get drawn in by the rich, buttery, crumbly center (as good as the best Chess Squares), but the cracking top with fennel and crunchy salt is why these savory circles won't leave your hands once you pick them up. This is what grown-up princesses serve at tea parties.

The malt in Lagunitas's Censored shines like malt powder in an ice cream shop frappe when combined with the cookies. The easy-drinking round brew lets the fennel and salt provide all the spice your mouth needs.

MAKES: 24 to 30 cookies
PAIRING: Lagunitas Brewing Company's Censored Rich Copper Ale
STYLE: Copper ales have what this cookie wants: malt without a big punch of hops.

4½ cups all-purpose flour

¾ cup sugar

½ teaspoon kosher salt

1½ cups (3 sticks) plus 2 tablespoons unsalted butter, cold

3 large egg yolks

2 tablespoons heavy cream

½ teaspoon vanilla extract

1 large egg

2½ tablespoons fennel seeds

2 teaspoons coarse sea salt

In the bowl of a stand mixer fitted with the paddle attachment, combine the flour, sugar, and salt and mix on low speed until combined. Add the butter and mix on medium-low speed until the mixture resembles coarse meal.

In a small bowl, whisk together the egg yolks, cream, and vanilla. With the mixer running on low speed, add the egg mixture. Raise the mixer speed to medium-low and mix until a cohesive dough forms, as long as 6 to 8 minutes.

Wrap the dough in plastic wrap and refrigerate for at least 1 hour. When ready to bake, let the dough sit at room temperature for 1 hour.

Preheat the oven to 350°F. Line a baking sheet with parchment paper.

In a small bowl, beat the egg to make an egg wash.

CONTINUED ⇢→

RICH BUTTER COOKIES WITH FENNEL SEED AND SEA SALT

CONTINUED

Scoop 2-teaspoon portions (or use a ¾-ounce ice cream scoop) of the dough and then roll them into balls and place them about 2 inches apart on the prepared baking sheet. Flatten each ball with the palm of your hand. Brush the tops of each cookie with the egg wash and then sprinkle generously with fennel seeds and sea salt. Bake the cookies for 15 minutes, or until the edges are light golden brown. Let cool for 5 minutes on the baking sheet, then transfer the cookies to a wire rack to cool completely.

The cookies will keep in an airtight container at room temperature for 2 to 3 days.

TIPS: Chill butter in the freezer for 30 minutes to get it extra cold.

OLIVE OIL & ALMOND BISCOTTI

DAVE CROFTON, One Girl Cookies
Brooklyn, New York

A crunch like a great crusty loaf gives way to a delicate, sleek inside that tastes just like the moment you bite into bread dredged through olive oil. In the midst of that moment are toasted almonds, the kind you imagine are served to passengers in first class. These biscotti don't suffer if you're eating them on their own, but they beg for something in a glass.

That glass should have Mother's Three Blind Mice—a medium-bodied brown beer that has caramel and chocolate notes to tease the sweetness and lemon out of the biscotti. You'll find yourself alternating sips and bites, each getting your mouth ready for the other.

MAKES: 42 to 48 cookies
PAIRING: Mother's Brewing Company's Three Blind Mice
STYLE: Opt for a brown ale. The middle-of-the-road character of brown beers will suit the silkiness of the olive oil and won't overwhelm the toasted nuttiness of the almonds.

1 cup whole unblanched almonds

2½ cups all-purpose flour

1 teaspoon baking powder

½ teaspoon salt

2 large eggs

Finely grated zest of 2 Meyer lemons or 1 standard lemon

1 cup sugar

½ cup extra-virgin olive oil

1 teaspoon vanilla extract

Fleur de sel or kosher salt, for finishing

Preheat the oven to 350°F. Line a baking sheet with parchment paper.

Place the almonds on an unlined baking sheet and roast for 18 minutes. The almonds should be well browned and fragrant. Remove and let cool; leave the oven on. When the almonds are cool enough to handle, carefully chop them into small pieces with a large knife or in a food processor.

Transfer the chopped almonds to a medium bowl and whisk together with the flour, baking powder, and salt. Set aside.

In the bowl of a stand mixer fitted with the paddle attachment, combine the eggs, lemon zest, sugar, oil, and vanilla. Mix on medium speed for 1 minute, until combined.

With the mixer running on low speed, gradually add the flour mixture to the egg mixture, stopping two or three times during mixing to scrape down the bowl. Mix until the dough is just beginning to come together.

Scoop the dough out onto the prepared baking sheet. The dough should be sticky. You may need to wet your hands slightly with water in order to work with it. Shape the dough into two equal logs, each about as wide as two knuckles on your middle finger and about ½ inch tall. Sprinkle a pinch of fleur de sel over each log.

Bake for 14 minutes, then rotate the baking sheet 180 degrees and bake for 14 minutes more. Let the logs cool for 12 to 15 minutes. Lower the oven temperature to 250°F.

Transfer the logs to a cutting board. Using a serrated knife, slice the logs into 1-inch-thick biscotti. Return the biscotti to the parchment paper–lined baking sheet, leaving ½ inch between each biscotti. Bake for 7 minutes, then rotate the baking sheet 180 degrees and bake for 7 minutes more, or until the biscotti are slightly crisp on the exposed sides. Transfer to a wire rack and let cool completely.

The biscotti will keep in an airtight container at room temperature for 2 to 3 days.

TIP: The stronger the flavor of your olive oil, the more it will shine through in this recipe.

CURRY COCONUT
MACAROONS

MOLLY YEH, *My Name Is Yeh*
Grand Forks, North Dakota

What if you could take everything you love about Thai food and just make it bite size? The macaroons here have their foundation in curry dishes and offer the same redolence and subtle smoothness that make it easy to stuff oneself. The coconut means this cookie fully straddles the line between sweet and savory, rendering it as seductive as kettle corn at a county fair.

The right partner for these nuanced cookies is Mikkeller's Jackie Brown. The brew from Denmark brings out the sweetness of the coconut at first and then pulls the curry out at the end. The lingering curry flavor is what will lead you to take bite after bite after bite. The beer gets brighter and more complex with each of those bites, and the brew's malty character provides caramel undertones to the coconut. Fans of sweet and salty alike will find something to love on their plate and in their glass.

MAKES: 10 to 15 cookies
PAIRING: Mikkeller's Jackie Brown
STYLE: An American brown ale will let the cookie shine and offer a touch more sweetness to balance the savory side of the macaroon.

2 cups sweetened shredded coconut

1 teaspoon curry powder

1 large egg white

Pinch of salt

Preheat the oven to 350°F. Line a baking sheet with parchment paper or a silicone baking mat.

In a small bowl, combine the coconut and curry powder. Stir the coconut until it's evenly coated with the curry powder.

In a clean large bowl, use a whisk to beat the egg white and salt until stiff peaks form. The peaks are stiff when you can hold your whisk upside down and the peaks hold their shape without collapsing. Gently fold the coconut and curry powder mixture into the egg white.

Spoon the dough onto the prepared baking sheet. If you like larger macaroons, you can use an ice cream scoop. The scoop yields 10 cookies, but they'll be perfect little half snowballs. You'll have about 15 cookies if you use a tablespoon.

Bake until golden brown, 13 to 15 minutes for larger macaroons and 10 to 12 minutes for smaller ones. Start checking the cookies after 10 minutes to make sure they don't burn. Let cool for 3 minutes on the baking sheet, then transfer to a wire rack to cool for 20 minutes.

The macaroons will keep in an airtight container at room temperature for about 1 week.

CHAI SPICE

KRISTY GREENWOOD, Victory Love + Cookies
Denver, Colorado

Sorry, baristas. The chai spice title belongs to this cookie. It gives you a tiny bit of heat, a little bit of sweet, and a spice blend that lingers just until you get the crunchy bits of sugar crystals. These cookies are a textural wonderland.

The Brunette Nut Brown is the other half of this flavor equation. Malty, nutty, and with a whisper of coffee (which is all you can think about once you hear "chai spice"), this brew elevates the spices in the cookie. You'll also get some caramel or toffee to bring a touch more sweetness to the pair.

MAKES: 72 cookies
PAIRING: Nebraska Brewing Company's Brunette Nut Brown
STYLE: Opt for brown ales (Nebraska's is an English-style brown ale) because they're content to let the spices in the cookie be the stars of the pairing.

6⅓ cups plus 2 tablespoons all-purpose flour

2 teaspoons cream of tartar

1 teaspoon baking soda

2 cups (4 sticks) unsalted butter, at room temperature

1½ cups confectioners' sugar

1 cup granulated sugar

3½ teaspoons ground ginger

2½ teaspoons ground cinnamon

1½ teaspoons ground cardamom

¼ teaspoon ground cloves

½ teaspoon kosher salt

¼ teaspoon freshly ground black pepper

Pinch of cayenne pepper

In a large bowl, combine the flour, cream of tartar and baking soda. Set aside.

In the bowl of a stand mixer fitted with the paddle attachment, cream together the butter, confectioners' sugar, granulated sugar, ginger, cinnamon, cardamom, cloves, kosher salt, black pepper, and cayenne until light and fluffy. Add the eggs, brandy, and vanilla paste. Mix well on medium speed, at least 2 minutes.

Add the flour mixture and mix just until uniform, about 1 minute. Cover and refrigerate for at least 2 hours.

Divide the dough into four equal pieces. Roll the pieces into logs about 1 inch high, 3 inches wide, and 14 inches long (about the size of a paper towel tube). Wrap them loosely in plastic wrap and then press down along the length of each log to turn it into an oblong shape. Refrigerate overnight or for up to 1 week.

Preheat the oven to 350°F. Line a baking sheet with parchment paper.

In a small bowl, combine the egg white with 1 teaspoon cold water to make an egg wash. Whisk vigorously.

Pour out a generous amount of turbinado sugar on a piece of parchment paper. Remove the plastic wrap from the dough and brush the entire surface with the egg wash. Press the dough into the sugar to coat on all sides. Cut the dough crosswise into ¼-inch slices. Place the slices on the prepared baking sheet and brush the tops with the egg wash and sprinkle more turbinado sugar on top. Bake for 12 to 14 minutes, until the surface of the cookies has ever so slightly puffed and looks dry but not brown. Let the cookies cool on the baking sheet for 5 minutes before transferring to a wire rack to cool completely.

The cookies will keep in an airtight container at room temperature for 3 to 5 days.

2 large eggs

2 tablespoons brandy

1 teaspoon vanilla paste

1 large egg white

Turbinado sugar (such as Sugar in the Raw), for coating

BATCH BAKEHOUSE'S
VANILLA BASIL SHORTIE

SUSAN LINLEY DETERING, Batch Bakehouse
Madison, Wisconsin

This tastes like you trapped spring in a cookie. The basil is vibrant, sitting on top of a cool bed of butter and vanilla. There's indulgence and lightness in the same bite because of the crunch of the cookie and the sumptuous buttercream inside.

The golden Kölsch is crisp and light, showcasing the cookie's richness without adding any weight to the pairing. The clean, approachable beer makes it easy to sit and sip and crunch and repeat.

MAKES: 24 sandwich cookies
PAIRING: One Barrel Brewing Company's Commuter Kölsch
STYLE: A Kölsch is a German brew that is crisp and clean, a nice bookend to the sweetness of the shortbread.

MOM'S SHORTBREAD COOKIES

1 bunch fresh basil, cut into thin ribbons

1½ cups (3 sticks) unsalted butter, at room temperature

1⅓ cups confectioners' sugar

3¼ cups all-purpose flour

½ teaspoon salt

1 teaspoon vanilla extract

REYNOLDS BUTTERCREAM FILLING

1 cup (2 sticks) unsalted butter, at room temperature

1 teaspoon vanilla extract

¼ teaspoon salt

1¾ cups confectioners' sugar

Confectioners' sugar, for dusting

To make the shortbread cookies, in the bowl of a stand mixer fitted with the paddle attachment, combine the basil, butter, confectioners' sugar, flour, salt, and vanilla. Mix on low speed until combined and large clumps form.

Place a sheet of plastic wrap on a flat surface. Turn out the dough onto the plastic wrap and divide it into two equal portions. Firmly roll each portion into a 2-inch-diameter log and wrap each tightly in plastic wrap. Refrigerate for at least 2 hours. The dough will keep for up to 2 weeks in the refrigerator and up to 2 months in the freezer. If frozen, allow the dough to thaw overnight in the refrigerator before baking.

Preheat the oven to 325°F. Line a baking sheet with parchment paper.

Cut the dough logs crosswise into ¼-inch slices. Place the slices about 1 inch apart on the prepared baking sheet. Bake for 15 to 18 minutes, until the edges are golden brown. Let the cookies cool on the baking sheet for 5 minutes before transferring to a wire rack to cool completely. The cookies must cool completely, a minimum of 20 minutes, before being assembled and decorated.

To make the buttercream filling, in the bowl of a stand mixer fitted with the paddle attachment, beat together the butter, vanilla, and salt on low speed until soft. Then, raise the mixer speed to high and beat until light and fluffy. Stop and scrape down the sides of the bowl three or four times. Add the confectioners' sugar, ¼ cup at a time, and beat on low or medium speed until incorporated. Once all the confectioners' sugar has been added, beat on high for 1 to 2 minutes, until the mixture is light and fluffy. The buttercream will lighten from cream to almost white in color. It will keep for up to 2 weeks in an airtight container in the refrigerator.

Divide the cooled cookies into pairs. With a small offset spatula, place a dollop of the buttercream in the center of the rough side of one cookie. Spread the buttercream evenly with a circular motion from the center toward the edge, leaving a small border uncovered. Place the second cookie on top of the buttercream and press the two cookies together. The buttercream will spread out to cover the rest of the cookie. Dust with confectioners' sugar.

The cookies will keep in an airtight container in the refrigerator for up to 1 week.

"One Barrel brews the way we bake—**ONE DELICIOUS BATCH AT A TIME**. We're neighbors, and I often stop for a quick drink on the way home WITH A COOKIE IN MY POCKET."

SUSAN LINLEY DETERING,
Batch Bakehouse

5

HOLIDAY

GINGER NIB
COOKIES • 75

ZIMTSTERNE
(WINTER STAR) • 76

POLVORONES • 79

RED TRUCK BAKERY'S
PERSIMMON COOKIES • 80

RUSSIAN
TEA CAKES • 82

NANA'S
MOLASSES COOKIES • 84

"Cookies offer up **QUICK HITS** of good flavors and fillings, including nuts and fruit. They offer a chance for *innovative*, *interesting*, and **EXPERIMENTAL** combinations in small quantities without having to make up a large cake."

Brian Noyes, owner
Red Truck Bakery

Cooler weather brings out some of the best in kitchens and breweries. Around the holidays, desserts have these naturally warming spices, like the cinnamon and nutmeg in the RED TRUCK BAKERY'S PERSIMMON COOKIES (page 80), or the kind of sweetness that makes my daughter ask if we can have powdered sugar for dinner. And there's A CAST OF MELLOW BREWS, able to calm the extremes and bring flavors together, just like your patient aunt who takes care of your fiery uncle when he's had a tad too much nog.

As half of an interfaith couple, I never thought about the idea that as Santa, I get to eat all the cookies on Christmas Eve, until we put out the plate for my daughter's first Christmas five years ago. (When you see her, be cool for a few more years.) My wife wraps and I eat. I love the holidays. If you make any of these before Christmas Eve, the only thing left for Santa will be store-bought. Sorry, Santa.

GINGER NIB COOKIES

MEGAN GARRELTS, pastry chef, Bluestem and Rye
Kansas City, Missouri

These cookies tickle your tongue with ginger, allspice, and cinnamon. With as much cocoa flavor as chocolate, this cookie beautifully melds together sweet and heat.

The Harvest Ale tames the cookie's fire for a brief moment, but the joy is in the finish, when the cinnamon and ginger come roaring back like a delicious hot pepper.

MAKES: 36 cookies
PAIRING: Goose Island Beer Company's Harvest Ale
STYLE: Look for an Extra Special Bitter (ESB). The English-style pale ale brings malt and some light fruit notes to the table that are great counterparts to the cookie's spice.

1¾ cups all-purpose flour

1 tablespoon plus 1 teaspoon unsweetened cocoa powder

1 teaspoon baking powder

1 teaspoon ground ginger

1 teaspoon ground cinnamon

1 teaspoon ground allspice

½ cup (1 stick) unsalted butter, at room temperature

½ cup firmly packed light brown sugar

⅓ cup blackstrap molasses

2 tablespoons dark beer (stout or porter)

1 large egg

2 tablespoons grated peeled fresh ginger

7 ounces dark chocolate, melted

½ cup granulated sugar

½ cup cocoa nibs

In a small bowl, whisk together the flour, cocoa powder, baking powder, ground ginger, cinnamon, and allspice. Set aside.

In the bowl of a stand mixer fitted with the paddle attachment, cream together the butter, brown sugar, and molasses. Add the beer, egg, and fresh ginger and mix until thoroughly combined. Slowly add the flour mixture. Fold in the melted chocolate. Cover and refrigerate to set the dough, about 1 hour.

Preheat the oven to 350°F. Line a baking sheet with parchment paper.

In a food processor, combine the granulated sugar and cocoa nibs and pulse until the cocoa nibs are slightly ground. Transfer the mixture to a medium bowl. Form 1-inch balls with the chilled cookie dough and roll them in the sugar—cocoa nib mixture. Place the coated dough balls on the prepared baking sheet 1 inch apart. Bake for 8 minutes. Transfer the cookies to a wire rack and let cool slightly.

The cookies are best eaten slightly warm, fresh from the oven, but they can be stored in an airtight container at room temperature for 2 to 3 days.

ZIMTSTERNE

(W I N T E R S T A R)

JOHN KRAUS, Patisserie 46
Minneapolis, Minnesota

With winter stars, it's like you're an archaeologist on holiday, who happens to uncover beautiful spiced almonds beneath a meringue-like layer of royal icing. These little cookies are powerfully sweet and spicy, but held in check by the clean lines of lemon that shine through each bite.

Beers change as they warm, with more flavors typically coming out after a few minutes in the glass. Here, a milk stout warms the cookie, providing creaminess and malty chocolate that make the party feel whole. Together, the winter stars and milk stout are like a cool drink of hot chocolate.

MAKES: 25 cookies
PAIRING: Dangerous Man Brewing Company's Chocolate Milk Stout
STYLE: A chocolate milk stout or milk stout will provide a creamy balance to the sweet icing and spicy cinnamon.

COOKIES

Butter, for greasing (optional)

4½ cups blanched almond flour, plus more as needed

2⅓ cups granulated sugar

3⅓ tablespoons ground cinnamon

Juice of 1 large lemon

½ large egg white

ROYAL ICING

3¾ cups confectioners' sugar

6 large egg whites

3 drops fresh lemon juice

Line two baking sheets with silicone baking mats or grease with butter.

To make the cookies, in the bowl of a stand mixer fitted with the paddle attachment, combine the almond flour, granulated sugar, cinnamon, and lemon juice. With the mixer running on low speed, slowly add the egg white until the dough is uniform.

On a flat surface, spread the dough so it is between ⅓ and ½ inch thick, the width of your index finger. If the dough won't spread, roll it in some almond flour to bind it together.

To make the royal icing, in a large bowl, use a whisk or a hand mixer to beat together the confectioners' sugar, egg whites, and lemon juice until stiff peaks form.

CONTINUED ON PAGE 78

ZIMTSTERNE (WINTER STAR)

Use a spatula to cover the dough completely with the royal icing. Cut cookies from the dough using a star-shaped cookie cutter. Use a butter knife to push on the interior edges of the cookie cutters if the dough sticks. Ice over any imperfections. Place the stars on the prepared baking sheets. Freeze the cookies on the baking sheets overnight.

Preheat the oven to 375°F.

Bake the chilled cookies for 5 to 7 minutes, until the corners are lightly browned.

The cookies will keep in an airtight container at room temperature for 2 days.

"I was **IN ALSACE, FRANCE,** one year shortly before Christmas when I tasted my first Zimtsterne cookie. Its nutty, chewy, cinnamon flavor brought me back to the smell of MY MOTHER'S KITCHEN during the holidays."

JOHN KRAUS, Patisserie 46

POLVORONES

ALEX RAIJ, Txikito
New York, New York

Polvorones give themselves over to your tongue. They melt slowly, the huge pop of confectioners' sugar receding quickly in the wave of bready almond crumbles.

The contrast alone between the snow white *polvorones* and the inky midnight of Flagship's Dark Mild is pleasing. But it's the ale's ability to match the sugar and almond subtext without stifling them that is key. This nice medium-bodied brew also has roasly and caramel notes that electrify the butter in the polvorones.

MAKES: 20 cookies
PAIRING: Flagship Brewing Company's Flagship Dark Mild
STYLE: English mild ales have a low hop profile (think less pine or citrus), a nice amount of body, and plenty of caramel or toffee notes that the beer can bring to the surface.

3 large egg yolks, at room temperature

½ cup plus 2 tablespoons semolina flour

½ cup all-purpose flour

5 tablespoons granulated sugar

½ cup (1 stick) plus 1 tablespoon unsalted butter, at room temperature

¼ teaspoon almond extract

1 teaspoon salt

⅓ cup blanched almond flour

Confectioners' sugar, for dusting

In a large bowl, whisk the egg yolks until mixed. Add the semolina flour, all-purpose flour, granulated sugar, butter, almond extract, salt, and almond flour. Mix by hand until the dough is uniform.

Line a baking sheet with parchment paper. Roll the dough into 1-inch balls and place them 1 inch apart on the prepared baking sheet. Press down lightly on the balls so they don't roll. Refrigerate the baking sheet for 1 hour.

Preheat the oven to 325°F.

Bake the cookies for 20 minutes, or until golden brown. The cookies will have a crumbly, shortbreadlike consistency. Let cool completely, then dust with confectioners' sugar. The cookies will keep in an airtight container at room temperature for up to 1 week.

RED TRUCK BAKERY'S
PERSIMMON COOKIES

BRIAN NOYES, Red Truck Bakery
Warrenton, Virginia

This cookie solves an age-old problem: the delicious but dry scone. The persimmon means that this sconelike cookie is moist and has a beautiful chew. It's why you'll find yourself craving it for breakfast. The raisins offer tiny pops of sweetness and the walnut gives the cookie a lovely textural contrast with a bit of crunch. These persimmon cookies are a wonderful hybrid of scones and trail mix.

Since these cookies feel right at breakfast time, a beer with coffee is a natural accompaniment. Founders Brewing Co.'s Breakfast Stout gives you a sumptuous java nose, deep hints of dark chocolate, and a lovely round finish that adds a nice little layer of deliciousness. The baked oats in the beer help to bring out the raisins in the same fashion as oatmeal. The beer has a comforting thickness that works with the biscuity cookie like a blanket over your shoulders and a hot cup of cocoa before you. Go ahead. Get warm.

MAKES: 20 to 24 cookies
PAIRING: Founders Brewing Co. Breakfast Stout
STYLE: The American double or imperial stout will have chocolate or coffee characteristics that blend nicely with the mild spice of this cookie.

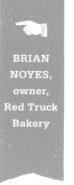

"The arrival of these homemade cookies, sent by my grandmother each fall and winter, was **ONE OF THE HIGHLIGHTS OF MY CHILDHOOD**. I haven't found any kid who doesn't like them—they have a good but subtle hint of holiday spices and are chock-full of raisins and walnuts. And, frankly, WE ENJOY THESE YEAR ROUND."

BRIAN NOYES, owner, Red Truck Bakery

Preheat the oven to 350F. Grease two baking sheets with butter.

Cut the top off the persimmons and squeeze the pulp into a glass or ceramic bowl, scraping the insides of the fruit with a spoon to get all the pulp. You will need ¾ cup pulp. (If you have extra, freeze it—just thaw to room temperature before using.) Set aside.

In a medium bowl, sift together the flour, baking soda, cloves, cinnamon, nutmeg, and salt. Set aside.

In a large bowl, cream together the butter and sugar until fluffy. (If you're mixing by hand, it will take about 5 minutes. Cut that number in half if you're using a hand mixer.)

Beat in the egg and the persimmon pulp until the color is uniform. Add the flour mixture and beat just until combined. The dough will be tan in color. Gently stir in the raisins and walnuts. Don't overmix.

Drop heaping tablespoons of the batter onto the prepared baking sheets about 1 inch apart. Bake for 15 minutes, or until lightly browned. Let cool slightly.

The cookies will keep in an airtight container at room temperature for about 1 week.

TIP: For best results, use local persimmons, which are usually available at farmers' markets (or from your neighbor's tree, if you ask nicely) in autumn after the first frost. Persimmons are very acidic until beyond ripe, so store them in a brown paper bag until they're extremely soft and squishy.

½ cup (1 stick) unsalted butter, at room temperature, plus more for the baking sheets

2 large American persimmons

2 cups all-purpose flour

1 teaspoon baking soda

½ teaspoon ground cloves

½ teaspoon ground cinnamon

½ teaspoon freshly grated nutmeg

½ teaspoon salt

1 cup sugar

1 large egg, at room temperature

1 cup raisins

1 cup chopped walnuts

★ RUSSIAN ★
TEA CAKES

TRACY MARCELLO, Odell Brewing Company
Fort Collins, Colorado

This cookie is a way for first-time bakers to shine. It's easy to make, but the resulting cookie is complex and lovely. These buttery drops melt in your mouth. They are crumbly and moist at the same time—these are why Julia Child loved butter. Silky bites of confectioners' sugar give way to crunchy pecans.

Smooth and creamy, the Odell amber ale enfolds the confectioners' sugar in the tea cakes. The brew's malt character complements the toasted pecans and the toffee characteristics just add more depth to the pairing. The beer and cookie share the same finish, a bit of caramel and nuttiness.

MAKES: 48 cookies
PAIRING: Odell 90 Shilling Ale
STYLE: Go for a light Scottish ale—it will bring caramel notes to the cookie, and the light hop profile will go well with the confectioners' sugar.

1 cup (2 sticks) unsalted butter, at room temperature

½ cup confectioners' sugar, plus more for rolling

1 teaspoon vanilla extract

2¼ cups all-purpose flour

¼ teaspoon salt

¾ cup pecans, finely chopped

Preheat the oven to 400°F.

In a large bowl, mix the butter, confectioners' sugar, and vanilla with a wooden spoon until combined, about 5 minutes. Add the flour, salt, and pecans. Continue mixing with the wooden spoon until a dough ball forms, about 6 minutes more.

Roll the dough into 1-inch balls and place them 2 to 3 inches apart on an ungreased baking sheet. Bake until set, but not browned, 10 to 12 minutes. Be careful to avoid burning on the bottom. Let cool on the baking sheet for 3 minutes, then transfer to a wire rack.

Spread some confectioners' sugar on a cutting board, enough to cover the surface evenly. Roll the still-warm (but not hot) cookies in the sugar and return them to the wire rack. Let cool for about 20 minutes, then roll again.

The cookies will keep in an airtight container at room temperature for up to 1 week.

NANA'S MOLASSES COOKIES

ROSHI MUNS, Society Bakery
Dallas, Texas

Your oven will be enrobed in the deep, rich scents of molasses and ginger, which will have you counting the minutes until the timer dings. These pillowy treats are the kind of cookie you make with your family, for your family. And just like Roshi Muns is drawn to the glass cookie jars on Julie Loller's kitchen counter (the Nana in this recipe), you'll find yourself sneaking back to break off pieces long after you're hungry.

We should call this pairing Christmas champagne. The pale ale becomes almost sparkly with an effervescent little pop of ginger. The beer and cookie share a delightful creaminess, while the citrus notes in the beer cut through the richness of the molasses for a bright finish. These two would share a toast if they weren't already in your belly.

MAKES: 48 to 54 cookies
PAIRING: Sierra Nevada Brewing Company's Pale Ale
STYLE: American pale ales have brightness that matches the depth and warmth of the cookie and a smooth, round finish.

4 cups all-purpose flour

4 teaspoons baking soda

1 teaspoon ground cloves

1 teaspoon ground ginger

2 teaspoons ground cinnamon

1 teaspoon salt

1½ cups vegetable shortening, plus more for the baking sheets

2 cups sugar, plus more for coating

½ cup original or mild molasses

3 large eggs

In a medium bowl, sift together the flour, baking soda, cloves, ginger, cinnamon, and salt. Set aside.

In a saucepan, melt the vegetable shortening over low heat, 8 to 10 minutes. The shortening should turn from a solid to a clear liquid. Place the saucepan on a trivet to cool for 20 to 30 minutes.

Transfer the cooled shortening to a large glass mixing bowl. Add the sugar, molasses, and eggs. Mix with a whisk or a hand mixer for 3 to 5 minutes.

Add the flour mixture. The batter will form a dense dough. Use a hand mixer to mix the batter for 4 to 6 minutes, alternating speeds, until the flour mixture is no longer visible. Cover the glass bowl with plastic wrap and refrigerate for at least 2 hours.

Position a rack in the center of the oven and preheat the oven to 375°F. Grease two baking sheets with vegetable shortening.

Spread an even layer of sugar (start with ½ cup and use more if you need it) on a cutting board, so that the board is not visible through the sugar.

Form the chilled dough into 1-inch balls. Roll them gently through the sugar to coat them. Then place them at least 2 inches apart on the prepared baking sheets. The cookies will spread and flatten. Bake for 10 minutes, until cracks begin to form in the center of the cookies. For crisper cookies with crispier edges, bake for 12 minutes.

Remove the baking sheets from the oven and let cool on a wire rack for 20 minutes.

The cookies will keep in an airtight container at room temperature for up to 1 week.

SPENT GRAIN

The first (and only) time I ever brewed beer, I helped make 1,200 gallons of oatmeal stout. The Free State Brewing Company is still standing in Lawrence, Kansas, but my career as a brewer there lasted a little less than eight hours.

The hitch was the spent grain—the wet malt or grain by-product created during the brewing process. As a pipe gushed brown grains into a bin, it was my job to use a garden hoe to rake it into an adjacent container set on the arms of a forklift. The only problem was that no matter how fast I shoveled, the grain kept coming.

As spent grain caked onto my forearms and the pipe seemed in danger of backing up, a full-time brewer jumped in to rescue me. I looked like I'd lost a fight with a cereal mascot. Less than half an hour later, the grains were on a loading dock waiting to be picked up by a local dairy.

Cows love spent grain. In fact, if you drink local milk with your cookies, you may very well have enjoyed milk produced by cows fed on spent grain. See, beer and milk aren't that far apart.

It's time we eliminated the middle cow. If you know a brewer, you may be able to score a small bag or two of spent grain, but because of how food and beverages are regulated and the sheer volume of what breweries produce (the few cups you need won't make a dent in the thousands of pounds they produce), it's likely easier to tap a home brewer. If you don't know anybody who makes beer in their kitchen, stop by a home-brewing store and explain that you want to do some baking with spent grains. You'll be up to your forearms in no time.

Spent grain is given to livestock, used for compost, and, in the case of the Alaska Brewing Company, fuels a steam boiler. It's incredibly versatile. The two recipes that follow, **COCONUT PORTER BEER PAWS** (page 88) and SPENT GRAIN AND CANDIED BACON WHOOPIE PIES (page 90), provide treats for the two- and four-legged friends in your house, but consider them a jumping-off point for spent grains, which are also great in pizza dough, bars, breads, biscuits, and, of course, cookies.

COCONUT PORTER BEER PAWS

CRYSTAL WIEBE, Beer Paws
Kansas City, Missouri

MAKES: ABOUT 24 DOG TREATS

5 slices bacon

3 cups spent porter grain

1½ cups all-purpose flour

2 large eggs

½ cup organic coconut oil,
at room temperature

¼ teaspoon ground cinnamon

Preheat the oven to 350°F. Line a baking sheet with parchment paper.

In a skillet or cast-iron pan, cook the bacon over medium-low heat until crispy. Eat the bacon or reserve it for another use. Pour the grease (about ¼ cup) into a large bowl.

Add the spent grain, flour, eggs, coconut oil, and cinnamon and mix with a spatula until all the ingredients are thoroughly combined.

Use a melon baller or teaspoon to drop the dough onto the prepared baking sheet. Flatten the scoops with a fork. Bake for 1 hour, rotating the baking sheet 180 degrees after 30 minutes. Lower the oven temperature to 275°F and bake for 1 hour more, or until the cookies are crisp. Transfer to a wire rack to cool.

The cookies will keep in airtight container at room temperature or in the refrigerator for up to 2 weeks.

SPENT GRAIN & CANDIED BACON WHOOPIE PIES

NEAL STEWART, Dogfish Head Craft Brewery
Milton, Delaware

MAKES: 10 WHOOPIE PIES

CANDIED BACON

1 cup firmly packed dark brown sugar

¼ teaspoon cayenne pepper

6 slices bacon

COOKIES

¼ cup (½ stick) unsalted butter, at room temperature

½ cup firmly packed dark brown sugar

¼ cup granulated sugar

2 large eggs

1 cup old-fashioned rolled oats

½ cup spent IPA grain

1 teaspoon vanilla extract

½ teaspoon baking soda

1 teaspoon salt

CANDIED BACON FILLING

½ cup (1 stick) unsalted butter

2½ cups confectioners' sugar

¼ cup Dogfish Head's Burton Baton (or any imperial IPA)

1 teaspoon vanilla extract

½ teaspoon salt

To make the candied bacon, preheat the oven to 350°F. Line a baking sheet with parchment paper.

Combine the brown sugar and cayenne in a medium flat-bottomed bowl. Coat each slice of bacon in the sugar mixture. Place the bacon on the prepared baking sheet. Bake for 10 minutes, or until the bacon is well caramelized. Set aside to cool; leave the oven on. Coarsely chop the bacon and set aside ¼ cup for the filling; reserve the rest for garnish.

To make the cookies, in the bowl of a stand mixer fitted with the paddle attachment, cream together the butter, brown sugar, and granulated sugar. Add the eggs one at a time and mix until light and fluffy.

In a food processor, grind ½ cup of the oats until fine. In a large bowl, combine the ground oats, remaining ½ cup oats, the spent grain, vanilla, baking soda, and salt. Add the oat mixture to the butter-sugar mixture and beat until combined.

Line a baking sheet with parchment paper. Use a 1-ounce scoop (2 heaping tablespoons) to drop portions of the cookie dough about 2 inches apart on the prepared baking sheet. Bake for 5 minutes, then rotate the sheet 180 degrees and bake for 5 minutes more. The tops of the cookies should be slightly firm to the touch.

To make the filling, in the bowl of a stand mixer fitted with the paddle attachment, cream together the butter and confectioners' sugar. Add the beer, vanilla, and salt. Mix until smooth. Fold in the reserved ¼ cup candied bacon with a spatula. Cover and refrigerate for 30 to 60 minutes, until the filling holds it shape.

Transfer the filling to a small resealable plastic bag. Seal it and cut off a bottom corner to create a piping bag. Spread the filling evenly over five cookies. Then place the remaining five cookies on top of the filling. Garnish with any leftover remaining candied bacon.

The cookies are best eaten the same day they're baked.

BEER

CARROT CAKE COOKIES
WITH TWO HEARTED ALE • 95

RYE IPA APRICOT
CRUMBLE BARS • 98

STONE SMOKED PORTER
MOCHA CHOCOLATE
CAKE COOKIES • 100

GINGERBREAD STOUT
COOKIES WITH BROWN
BUTTER STOUT GLAZE • 102

VANILLA BEAN BUFFALO SWEAT
COOKIES • 105

GINGER LEMON RADLER
COOKIES • 107

CHOCOLATE TART CHERRY
STOUT COOKIES • 109

"You need only **TWO HANDS** and no silverware, one hand for your *beer* and the other for your *cookie*."

DAVID MUNRO, Bell's Brewery, Inc.

If you've come this far, maybe you're willing to go a little farther. Now, we're going to go ahead and put the beer in the cookies. And drink beer with those cookies that have beer in them. If it sounds a bit beer-y, don't worry. The end result is some slamming cookies.

Beer, it turns out, is the base ingredient in culinary alchemy. Just as the RYE IPA APRICOT CRUMBLE BARS (page 98) let you re-create jam-slathered toast, the BEER-BASED COOKIES in this chapter will bring to mind carrot cake, vanilla wafers, café mocha, chocolate-dipped cherries, gingerbread cinnamon rolls, and savory doughnuts. The beer in cookie and liquid forms, when reunited on your taste buds, activate their Wonder Twins deliciousness powers.

CARROT CAKE COOKIES
WITH TWO HE♥RTED ALE

DAVID MUNRO, Bell's Brewery, Inc.
Kalamazoo, Michigan

These are a gateway to becoming a carrot cake addict. Moist and delicate, these sandwich cookies are a shining balance of fruit and nuts. Like a perfect background singer, a touch of grapefruit in the filling (the addictive part) brings out a hint of citrus in the beer-soaked raisins.

Carrot cake and IPAs are great dessert partners because the cake tones down the brew's hoppiness and the beer keeps the cake from being too sweet. The two are well balanced in this innovative take on a classic beer and dessert pairing.

MAKES: 54 to 60 sandwich cookies
PAIRING: Bell's Brewery, Inc.'s Two Hearted Ale
STYLE: An American IPA will have lots of hop intensity, floral notes, and a bit of citrus that cuts through the rich cream cheese–stuffed carrot cookies.

FILLING

12 ounces cream cheese

¾ cup (1½ sticks) unsalted butter, at room temperature

3 cups confectioners' sugar

2 teaspoons vanilla extract

½ teaspoon salt

2 teaspoons finely grated grapefruit zest

1 teaspoon fresh grapefruit juice

To make the filling, in the bowl of a stand mixer fitted with the paddle attachment, cream together the cream cheese, butter, and confectioners' sugar until light and fluffy, 6 to 8 minutes. Add the vanilla, salt, grapefruit zest, and grapefruit juice and mix until combined. Transfer to an airtight container and refrigerate overnight.

To make the cookies, soak the raisins in the ale for at least 2 hours.

Meanwhile, in the bowl of a stand mixer fitted with the paddle attachment, beat together the butter, brown sugar, granulated sugar, salt, and vanilla. Start on the lowest speed, then after a minute raise the speed to medium. Cream until light and fluffy, 4 to 5 minutes.

CONTINUED ▸⟶

CARROT CAKE COOKIES
WITH TWO HEARTED ALE

CONTINUED

COOKIES

3 cups raisins

1 (12-ounce) bottle Bell's Two Hearted Ale (or any American IPA)

1½ cups (3 sticks) unsalted butter, at room temperature

2¼ cups plus 2 tablespoons firmly packed dark brown sugar

1½ cups granulated sugar

½ teaspoon salt

2 teaspoons vanilla extract

3 large eggs, at room temperature

3 cups whole wheat flour

2 cups plus 2½ tablespoons all-purpose flour

1½ teaspoons baking soda

1½ teaspoons baking powder

1 tablespoon ground allspice

5 cups plus 2 tablespoons finely grated carrots

3⅓ plus 1 tablespoon old-fashioned rolled oats

3 cups sweetened finely shredded coconut

2½ cups coarsely chopped walnuts

In a small bowl, beat the eggs. With the mixer running on low speed, slowly add the beaten eggs to the butter mixture. Scrape down the sides of the bowl in between additions of egg.

In a large bowl, sift together the whole wheat flour, all-purpose flour, baking soda, baking powder, and allspice. With the mixer running on low speed, add the flour mixture 1 cup at a time until combined.

Drain the beer-soaked raisins in a sieve in the sink. Blot them with a paper towel to remove any excess liquid. Drain the shredded carrots in the same fashion. Excess juice will lead to soft dough.

With a wooden spoon, mix the raisins and carrots into the dough by hand. Add the oats, coconut, and walnuts and mix until evenly distributed. Cover the bowl with plastic wrap and refrigerate for 1 hour.

Preheat the oven to 350°F. Line a baking sheet with parchment paper.

Place 1-tablespoon (roughly 1-ounce) scoops of the dough about 1½ inches apart on the prepared baking sheet. Bake for 8 minutes, then rotate the baking sheet 180 degrees and bake for 4 to 6 minutes more, until the tops are firm. Let cool on the baking sheet for 1 to 2 minutes, then transfer to a wire rack. Once completely cool to the touch, transfer to an airtight container and leave overnight.

Remove the cream cheese filling from the fridge 1 hour before you want to make the cookies. With a knife, spread an even layer of the filling from the center to nearly the edge of the flat side of one cookie. Place another cookie atop the filling.

The cookies will keep in an airtight container in the refrigerator for 2 days.

RYE IPA APRICOT CRUMBLE BARS

ANNE CROY, Pastaria
St. Louis, Missouri

Close your eyes and think about a fat slice of crusty rye bread. It's perfectly toasted, the edges slightly brown, with a fat pat of butter and a thick spread of chunky apricot jam on top. This bar cookie is a lovely, thoughtful take on rye toast and jam, exactly what you hope arrives on the plate at diners and brunch spots alike.

Like a great Jewish deli, this pairing can never get enough rye. 4 Hands Divided Sky Rye amps up the rye in the shortbread and crumble and dances alongside the lemon zest thanks to the brew's own citrus and grapefruit notes.

MAKES: 24 cookies
PAIRING: 4 Hands Brewing Co.'s Divided Sky Rye IPA
STYLE: Rye beers (IPA or otherwise) will amplify the rye and caraway seeds in the bar cookies and tease out a bit of sweetness from the apricot filling.

RYE IPA APRICOT COMPOTE

12 ounces dried apricots, chopped into ¼-inch bits

1½ cups 4 Hands Brewing Divided Sky Rye IPA (or any rye IPA)

¼ cup maple sugar

1 cup apricot purée

Zest of 1 large lemon, finely grated

To make the compote, preheat the oven to 350°F.

Place the apricots, beer, and maple sugar in a 9 by 13-inch baking dish. Roast for 1½ hours, or until the apricots have swelled and softened and the liquid has thickened to a syrup. Let cool slightly.

In a food processor, pulse the dried apricot mixture with the apricot purée and lemon zest until thick and still slightly chunky. Set aside to cool.

To make the rye shortbread, in the bowl of a stand mixer fitted with the paddle attachment, cream together the butter and confectioners' sugar until light and fluffy. Add the vanilla and mix until incorporated. Add the all-purpose flour, rye flour, and salt and mix until fully combined. Pat the dough into a disc and wrap it in plastic wrap. Refrigerate for at least 30 minutes.

Preheat the oven to 350°F.

Roll out the dough to fit the bottom of a 9 by 13-inch baking dish. Bake for 15 minutes. Let cool slightly. Increase the oven temperature to 400°F and position a rack in the upper third.

To make the crumble, in a food processor, pulse the flour, brown sugar, salt, and ground caraway seeds. Add the cubed butter. Pulse until chunks begin to form. Scoop the mixture into a large bowl and mix in the chopped walnuts. Set aside.

Spread the apricot compote on top of the cooled shortbread. Spread the nut crumble on top of the fruit layer. Bake for 12 minutes, or until the crumble is set and beginning to brown. Lower the oven temperature to 350°F and bake for 12 minutes more. Let cool completely and cut into 24 squares. Don't wrap or cover tightly, as the crumble will soften. Serve the same day.

RYE SHORTBREAD

1 cup (2 sticks) unsalted butter, at room temperature

¾ cup confectioners' sugar

2 teaspoons vanilla extract

1 cup all-purpose flour

1 cup rye flour

1 teaspoon salt

CARAWAY BLACK WALNUT CRUMBLE

1 cup all-purpose flour

⅔ cup firmly packed dark brown sugar

¼ teaspoon salt

¼ teaspoon ground caraway seeds

1 cup (2 sticks) unsalted butter, cold, cut into cubes

1 cup black walnuts, coarsely chopped

STONE·SMOKED·PORTER
MOCHA CHOCOLATE CAKE
· C O O K I E S ·

SABRINA LOPICCOLO, Stone Brewing Company
Escondido, California

This cookie is what bubble bath commercials have always promised: rich, deep, and sensual. It's got a moist, chocolate cake heart that gets roundness and a touch of smoke from the porter. The espresso is just strong enough to come through at the end alongside the semisweet chocolate.

The first sip of Stone's Imperial Russian Stout jump-starts the chocolate in the brew and the cookie. But just when you think it will be too rich, the shared coffee characteristics blend in the finish to cleanse your palate.

MAKES: 36 cookies
PAIRING: Stone Imperial Russian Stout
STYLE: Imperial stouts will have coffee and chocolate notes that echo what you'll taste in the cookie.

1 cup Stone Smoked Porter (or any smoked porter)

1 tablespoon ground espresso

2½ cups all-purpose flour

⅓ cup unsweetened cocoa powder

1 teaspoon baking soda

¼ teaspoon kosher salt

1 cup granulated sugar

¾ cup firmly packed dark brown sugar

1 cup (2 sticks) unsalted butter, at room temperature

3 large eggs

2 cups semisweet chocolate chips

In a small saucepan, heat the beer until warm to the touch. Don't let the beer boil. Remove the pan from the heat and stir in the ground espresso. Cover with plastic wrap and steep for 30 minutes.

Preheat the oven to 300°F.

In a medium bowl, whisk together the flour, cocoa powder, baking soda, and salt. Set aside.

In the bowl of a stand mixer fitted with paddle attachment, blend together the sugars and butter to form a grainy paste. Scrape down the sides of the bowl as necessary.

Pour the beer through a strainer into a small bowl to filter out the espresso grounds; discard the espresso grounds. Add 3 tablespoons of beer and the eggs to the stand mixer. Mix on medium speed until smooth. Add the flour mixture and chocolate chips. Mix on low speed until just combined. Don't overmix.

Drop rounded tablespoons of the dough 2 inches apart on an ungreased baking sheet. Bake for 15 to 18 minutes, until the tops of the cookies are slightly firm to the touch. Let cool on the baking sheets for 5 minutes, then transfer to a wire rack.

The cookies will keep in an airtight container at room temperature for up to 2 weeks.

GINGERBREAD STOUT COOKIES with BROWN BUTTER STOUT GLAZE

CHELSEA WILLIAMS, Chelsea's Bakehaus
Kansas City, Missouri

The soul of a gingerbread cinnamon roll lives within this cookie. The soft, thick gingerbread has a pleasant spiciness beneath a gorgeous coat of icing. The butter and stout in the icing give it body and enough of a savory twist to perfectly match the gingerbread.

A Belgian dark ale is well suited to this complex cookie. It's a boozy flirt, teasing you with different hints of rum and cocoa. But the best characteristic is its ability to enfold the gingerbread and icing. The finish is smooth like port.

MAKES: several dozen cookies
PAIRING: Unibroue's Trois Pistoles
STYLE: A Belgian strong dark ale will bring some savory notes to this cookie and has enough body to match the ginger in the cookie and sugar in the glaze.

COOKIES

5½ cups all-purpose flour

1½ tablespoons ground ginger

2 teaspoons ground cinnamon

½ teaspoon ground allspice

¼ teaspoon ground cloves

1½ teaspoons baking soda

¼ cup stout

1 cup molasses

1 cup (2 sticks) unsalted butter

1 cup granulated sugar

½ cup firmly packed dark brown sugar

1 large egg

To make the cookies, in a large bowl, whisk together the flour, ginger, cinnamon, allspice, and cloves. Set aside.

In a small bowl, whisk the baking soda into the stout until smooth. Whisk in the molasses.

In the bowl of a stand mixer fitted with the paddle attachment, cream together the butter, granulated sugar, and brown sugar until light and fluffy. Add the egg and mix well, scraping down the sides of the bowl as necessary. With the mixer on low, alternate between adding the flour mixture and the molasses mixture, beginning and ending with the flour mixture. Wrap the dough in plastic wrap and refrigerate for at least 1 hour.

CONTINUED ON PAGE 104

GINGERBREAD STOUT COOKIES WITH BROWN BUTTER STOUT GLAZE

CONTINUED

BROWN BUTTER STOUT GLAZE

¼ cup (½ stick) unsalted butter

2 cups confectioners' sugar

3 tablespoons stout

While the dough is chilling, make the glaze. In a small saucepan, melt the butter over medium heat. Simmer until it becomes a rich golden brown color. Remove from the heat and let it cool.

In a medium bowl, combine the cooled brown butter, confectioners' sugar, and stout. Whisk until thick, smooth, and glossy. Cover the surface of the glaze with plastic wrap and set aside on the counter.

Preheat the oven to 350°F. Line a baking sheet with parchment paper.

Lightly dust your work surface with flour. Using your hands, shape the dough into a flat layer about ¼ inch thick. With your cookie cutter of choice, cut out shapes and place them 1 inch apart on the prepared baking sheet. Bake for 10 to 12 minutes, until the edges and tops are firm to the touch. Transfer the cookies to a wire rack, with a piece of parchment or plastic wrap underneath, to cool. Use a spoon to glaze the tops of the slightly warm cookies.

Let the cookies cool completely to set the glaze

They're great the next day and will keep in an airtight container at room temperature for about 1 week.

VANILLA BEAN BUFFALO SWEAT COOKIES

JEFF GILL, founder, Tallgrass Brewing Company
Manhattan, Kansas

This is the vanilla wafer, all grown up. Crunchy toasted edges and the crackling raw sugar on this cookie meld into a luscious vanilla. Yet thanks to the beer, the center stays soft. My only wish is that every bar would have a jar of these beauties right next to the taps.

This cookie wants more of the beer that helped make it. The Vanilla Bean Buffalo Sweat brings a really pleasing creaminess to the pair. It also supercharges the vanilla within the cookie, thanks to some dark espresso characteristics, and makes the turbinado sugar sing like Pop Rocks.

MAKES: 12 to 15 cookies
PAIRING: Tallgrass Brewing Company's Vanilla Bean Buffalo Sweat
STYLE: Grab an oatmeal cream stout. The slightly sweet stout will play off the cookie's savory elements.

½ cup (1 stick) unsalted butter, at room temperature, plus more for the baking sheets

1 teaspoon baking soda

½ teaspoon salt

1 large egg

1 cup firmly packed dark brown sugar

2 cups all-purpose flour

4 ounces Tallgrass Vanilla Bean Buffalo Sweat (substitute milk or sweet stout)

2 tablespoons turbinado sugar (such as Sugar in the Raw)

Preheat the oven to 350°F. Grease a pair of baking sheets with butter.

In a large bowl, using a wooden spoon, mix the baking soda, salt, egg, butter, brown sugar, and 1 cup of the flour until consistently creamy brown, 2 to 3 minutes. Add the beer and the remaining 1 cup flour. Mix thoroughly for 2 to 3 minutes more, until the dough is consistently creamy and a bit lighter brown in color.

Place 1-teaspoon dollops of the dough 1½ to 2 inches apart on the prepared baking sheets. The cookies will flatten while baking. Before putting the baking sheets in the oven, generously sprinkle turbinado sugar on top of the cookies. Bake for 14 minutes, until the cookies are dark golden brown. The edges will be crispy.

The cookies will keep in an airtight container at room temperature for up to 1 week.

ginger lemon radler cookies

CARLENE SCHIPFMANN, Boulevard Brewing Company
Kansas City, Missouri

Here's the recipe for how you fall in love with beer: Mix it gently with citrus and sugar in a bready, luscious cookie. These are "hide them, please" addictive because of the rising sweetness that acts as the bliss point for beer cookies. The finish is smooth like a doughnut with just enough dryness to need a cold beer to wash it down.

That cold beer should be Boulevard's Tank 7, a Belgian-style farmhouse ale with lots of lemon and grapefruit in the nose and body. The brilliant citrus notes lead into a peppery finish, the perfect answer to the sugar in the cookies.

MAKES: 36 cookies
PAIRING: Boulevard Brewing Company's Tank 7
STYLE: Look for a saison or farmhouse ale. Both will have fruit and citrus characteristics, as well as a dry finish that is dynamite with this cookie.

2¼ cups all-purpose flour

1 teaspoon baking powder

½ cup Boulevard Ginger Lemon Radler, Boulevard Zon, or Stiegl Radler

½ cup extra-virgin olive oil

½ cup sugar

½ tablespoon finely grated lemon zest (optional)

1 tablespoon finely chopped candied ginger (optional)

In a medium bowl, whisk together the flour and baking powder. Set aside.

In a large glass bowl, combine the beer, olive oil, sugar, lemon zest, and candied ginger and mix with a hand mixer on medium speed until combined.

Gradually add the flour mixture to the radler mixture. Blend together on medium speed until a soft dough, about the consistency of pizza dough, forms. Cover the bowl with plastic wrap and refrigerate for at least 2 hours or up to overnight.

Preheat the oven to 350°F. Line two baking sheets with parchment paper.

CONTINUED ▸⟶

GINGER LEMON RADLER COOKIES

CONTINUED

Drop rounded tablespoons of the dough ½ inch apart on the prepared baking sheets and gently flatten the dough. (Alternatively, roll about 1 tablespoon of dough with your palm to form a 4-inch-long, ½-inch-wide rope. Pinch the ends of the rope together to form a circle.)

Bake for 18 to 20 minutes, until the tops of the cookies are firm to the touch and the bottoms are golden brown. Transfer the cookies to a wire rack to cool completely.

The cookies can be stored in an airtight container at room temperature for up to 2 weeks, or frozen for up to 3 months.

Chocolate Tart Cherry Stout Cookies

4 HANDS BREWING COMPANY
St. Louis, Missouri

Somewhere in Cake Land, a dark chocolate–covered cherry crash-lands in a moist bed of chocolate cake. And your mouth has the good fortune to uncover it. Chocolate Tart Cherry Stout Cookies have an easy, round sweetness that is effortlessly satisfying. The beer goes swimmingly with the cookie: The cocoa nibs in the chocolate milk stout make the chocolate and cherry dazzle. And in this case, the cookies leave you with the happiest by-product of baking with beer: an opened beer that you need to drink.

MAKES: 28 to 30 cookies
PAIRING: 4 Hands Brewing Co.'s Chocolate Milk Stout
STYLE: Milk stouts will let the chocolate and cherry sing. You can substitute the milk stout you're drinking with the beer for the recipe, as well.

1½ cups sifted cake flour

¼ cup unsweetened cocoa powder

½ teaspoon salt

½ teaspoon baking soda

1 teaspoon baking powder

1 cup semisweet chocolate chips

½ cup (1 stick) unsalted butter, at room temperature

½ cup firmly packed light brown sugar

¼ cup granulated sugar

1 tablespoon molasses

1 teaspoon vanilla extract

1 large egg

6 ounces 4 Hands Chocolate Milk Stout (or any chocolate milk stout)

1 cup dried tart cherries

Preheat the oven to 350°F. Line a baking sheet with parchment paper.

In a large bowl, combine the cake flour, cocoa, salt, baking soda, baking powder, and chocolate chips. Mix together with a spatula until combined.

In the bowl of a stand mixer fitted with the paddle attachment, cream together the butter, brown sugar, and granulated sugar. Add the molasses, vanilla, and egg. Mix until combined. Add the flour mixture. With the mixer running on low speed, add the beer. Fold in the tart cherries last, mixing until the dough is uniform.

Place heaping tablespoons of the dough about 2 inches part on the prepared baking sheet. Bake for 15 minutes, until the tops of the cookies are firm to the touch. Transfer to a wire rack to cool completely.

The cookies will keep in an airtight container at room temperature for 3 to 5 days.

CONTRIBUTORS

4 Hands Brewing Co.

4 Hands Brewing Co., located in the LaSalle Park neighborhood of St. Louis, Missouri, provides the craft beer enthusiast a handcrafted portfolio, inspired by the American craft movement, that pushes the limits of creativity. The use of wine and spirit barrels containing an array of fruit, herbs, and spices in conjunction with wild yeast strains enhances the flavors to produce a one-of-a-kind beer. For more information, visit 4handsbrewery.com.

Bakery Lorraine

Jeremy Mandrell and Anne Ng met while working for Thomas Keller at Bouchon Bakery in the Napa Valley, California, and have been baking together ever since. The husband-and-wife duo honed their skills in different kitchens around the San Francisco Bay Area before moving to San Antonio in the summer of 2010. In 2011, they established Bakery Lorraine, through which they wish to share their craftsmanship with you. Every item they put out is handmade with the utmost care and attention to detail. Each ingredient is treated with the proper respect and thoughtfulness it deserves—from the miller's flour to the dairy farmer's eggs and butter.

Batch Bakehouse

Batch Bakehouse, a neighborhood bakery, opened its doors in Madison, Wisconsin, in 2009. Each morning, the bakers hand-shape loaf breads and roll classic French baguettes and get to work on filling the pastry case with croissants, cookies, scones, and tarts.

Amy Beeman

After studying English at the University of Missouri, Amy moved back home to Kansas City and worked for a nonprofit consulting firm, McKellar Consulting. Planning fund-raising events for clients was the most enjoyable part of her job, since she was able to work with catering companies to plan menus. It was during this time that Amy found her true passion for food, and she began spending her free time catering events.

Her hobby turned into a career when Amy began working at Kansas City's Dolce Bakery. After four years at Dolce Bakery, Amy moved with her husband to Boston, where she was hired as executive pastry chef at South End Buttery. Always starting with quality ingredients, Amy likes to keep her pastries simple and subtle. Sweet and savory flavors are combined with a touch of whimsy to tickle and please the palate. The style of South End Buttery is a perfect fit for Amy, presenting food that is not fussy but familiar, contemporary but approachable.

Stacy Begin

Stacy Begin is the owner of Two Fat Cats Bakery in Portland, Maine. Stacy spent twenty years in the nonprofit field before establishing Blackbird Baking Company of Maine, an in-home bakery specializing in pies and breakfast pastries. In 2012, Stacy and her husband, Matthew Holbrook, purchased Two Fat Cats Bakery and continue the bakery's legacy of American baking from scratch. The bakery has been featured in *Bon Appétit*, *Downeast* magazine, the *Dispatch*, and the *Boston Globe*, as well as on the Food Network.

Erin Brown

In 2007, Erin Brown opened Dolce Bakery in Prarie Village, Kansas, with a commitment to "feeding the people with love." That means no shortcuts, no mixes, and nothing phoned in. Dolce is a modern expression of baking tradition —a bright, warm café where her aunt's cinnamon roll recipe delights new generations alongside Erin's cakes, cookies, and other signature creations. The perfect place to pause for a moment of handcrafted happiness or grab some goodies to go.

Frank Carollo & Amy Emberling

Frank Carollo and Amy Emberling are the co-owners of Zingerman's Bakehouse, an artisanal bakery in Ann Arbor, Michigan, and a member of Zingerman's Community of Businesses. They've been working together for the twenty-two years of the bakery's history. Frank and Amy have each had a love of great food since their childhoods, enjoying the ethnic foods of their respective families. They have an equally strong commitment to working with people in an enriching and fun work environment. They spend their days trying to bake the most flavorful baked goods possible with their community of bakers.

Anne Croy

Anne Croy is the executive pastry chef at Pastaria Restaurant in St. Louis, Missouri. There, she pursues her vision that simple, quality ingredients can be transformed and elevated into the extraordinary in an environment that is both unassuming and welcoming.

She became interested in cooking at an early age while spending summers on her father's family farm in rural Oklahoma.

Their decision to live sustainably or grow without chemicals was neither nouveau nor trendy, but simply a creative necessity. It was here that the seeds of her passions grew. As a fine arts student, she supported herself by cooking in restaurant and catering kitchens. After a twenty-two-year career as an art director in the furniture and design industry, she sought a new creative outlet. She now works to transform classic American and European pastries, breads, and desserts. She loves working with whole grains and easily moves from sweet to savory.

Dogfish Head Craft Brewery

Dogfish Head Craft Brewery makes off-centered ales for off-centered people. Since 1995, Dogfish has brewed with nonstandard ingredients such as raisins, chicory, maple syrup, and grapes, changing the way people think about beer. Dogfish Head believes beer can have as much flavor, complexity, diversity, food compatibility, and ageability as the world's finest wines. To discover your favorite off-centered ale, visit www.dogfish.com.

Abbey-Jo and Josh Eans

After finding much culinary success at Kansas City hot spots like The Drop Bar & Bistro, Blanc Burgers + Bottles, and The American Restaurant, Abbey-Jo Eans and her husband, Josh, purchased their "favorite spot on Sunday morning to get breakfast"— Happy Gillis Café & Hangout. As chefs and parents of three children, the purchase of a restaurant that serves breakfast and lunch was an opportunity to stay in the restaurant business while still seeing their children at night. Their seasonally changing menu reflects their support for local farmers and retailers, as well as a dedication to simple, wholesome ingredients. The Eans family lives in the same community as Happy Gillis in the Columbus Park neighborhood near the River Market.

Christopher Elbow Artisanal Chocolate

Chocolatier Christopher Elbow's culinary career began at the Lincoln Country Club in 1992 while he was a student at the University of Nebraska. After heading the kitchen at Shiraz in Kansas City, he helped Emeril Lagasse open Delmonico Steakhouse at the Venetian and Jean Joho open the Eiffel Tower Restaurant at the Paris Resort and Casino in Las Vegas, Nevada. He returned to Kansas City, where he was the pastry chef at The American. There, he began to perfect his chocolate-making skills before opening his own chocolate shop in 2004. Six years later, he opened Glace, an artisan ice cream shop with two locations in the Kansas City area.

Megan Garrelts

A graduate of the Culinary Institute of America, Megan Garrelts worked under Gale Gand at Tru and alongside Megan Romano at Charlie Palmer's Aureole in the Mandalay Bay Hotel. After serving as the executive pastry chef at the Getty Center Restaurant in Los Angeles, she moved to Kansas City and opened Bluestem with her husband, Colby Garrelts, in 2004. The duo opened Rye, a celebration of Midwest cuisine, in Leawood, Kansas, in 2012. They've also authored a pair of cookbooks, *Bluestem: The Cookbook* and *Made in America*.

Jeff Gill

A former geologist, Jeff Gill turned his love of homebrewing into his vocation when he opened the Tallgrass Brewing Company with his wife, Tricia, in 2007. The brewery in Manhattan, Kansas, launched with Pub Ale, and has since added Buffalo Sweat Oatmeal Cream Stout, 8-Bit American Pale Ale, and Velvet Rooster, a Belgian-style tripel, to its year-round lineup. In 2010, the Tallgrass made the decision to produce its beer exclusively in cans. The brewery has a major expansion and brewpub downtown planned for 2015.

Natasha Goellner

Margaret Braun's *Cakewalk* set Natasha Goellner on the path to pastry. A graduate of the French Culinary Institute in 2004, Goellner launched her own wedding cake business in Kansas City. A year later, the wedding cake business evolved into Natasha's Mulberry & Mott—a bakery that made cakes, pastries, and ice cream. In short order, she became known for producing delicate and colorful French macarons. In 2014, Goellner launched LanMou Chocolates, a confectionery company, with Megan Piel.

Kristy Greenwood

Kristy Greenwood was working as a baker and manager for the Denver Bread Company in 2006 when she was diagnosed with cancer. After taking a few years to recuperate and think about what she wanted to do with her life, Greenwood realized that baking was her passion. In 2008, Victory Love + Cookies was born and Greenwood began selling cookies at the Denver Bread Company's retail counter. She hopes to get her cookies out into the world, spreading love and light, sugar and flavor, by whatever means necessary.

Sofia Varanka Hudson
Sofia Varanka Hudson is an avid cook and enjoys experimenting with unexpected flavors in baking. She owns Swoon, a sugar cookie company in Kansas City, Missouri, where the cookies are based on her mother-in-law's recipes.

John Kraus
John Kraus found his calling working with the *boulangers* at the Dorchester Hotel in London, England. The ritual of high tea and the precision of the pastry served appealed to the exacting young chef. Before returning to the United States, Kraus served on staff for the opening of the Michelin-starred restaurant Fleur de Sel. Then, he worked in pastry for Chef Robert Wagner at Wild Boar in Nashville, Tennessee, and was named executive pastry chef at Magnolia Restaurant in Chicago, Illinois.

In 1999, he joined the French Pastry School, where he would rise to the rank of chef de cuisine over the course of a decade. Three years later, he was named the Paris Gourmet Pastry Chef of the Year and the Valrhona National Dessert Champion. In 2010, Kraus opened Patisserie 46, a French bakery in Minneapolis, Minnesota, where neighbors and visitors are invited to sit down and connect over bread, pastries, confections, and coffee.

Amy Lemon
Amy Lemon, pastry chef of Emeril's Delmonico and NOLA restaurants, originally joined Emeril's Delmonico in 2006 as its assistant pastry chef. Born in Langley, Virginia, Lemon spent most of her early childhood in Europe—Holland and Germany—while her father was in the Air Force, before moving to southern California when she was twelve. Lemon's multicultural background expanded her palate, introducing her to a spectrum of flavors and techniques. In the United States, however, she couldn't find the same types of cuisine she had enjoyed in Europe. Lemon began working in the hospitality industry as a hostess while in high school. She worked in the front of the house for a few years before moving into the kitchen, where she felt more creative. She graduated from the Art Institute of Santa Monica in 2000 with a degree in culinary arts before working in the pastry departments at Patina in Los Angeles and Higgins in Portland, Oregon. At Emeril's Delmonico and NOLA, Lemon and her pastry team follow an ingredient-driven philosophy, using the season's freshest and local products to re-create classic New Orleans flavors.

J. Kenji Lopéz-Alt
J Kenji Lopéz-Alt is the managing culinary director of *Serious Eats* and author of the James Beard Award–nominated column "The Food Lab," where he unravels the science of home cooking. A restaurant-trained chef and former editor at *Cook's Illustrated* magazine, he is the author of upcoming *The Food Lab: Better Home Cooking Through Science*, to be released by W. W. Norton.

Tracy Marcello

Tracy Marcello is the marketing and communications coordinator for Odell Brewing Company in Fort Collins, Colorado. She loves to bake and cook with craft beer, and frequently posts her favorite recipes on the brewery blog at www.odellbrewing.com/blog.

Kate & Scott Meinke

Kate and Scott Meinke opened the Heirloom Bakery & Hearth, a home-style, community-oriented eatery where everything is made from scratch using local and seasonal ingredients whenever possible, in Kansas City's Brookside neighborhood in 2015.

Scott Meinke began baking professionally at the Spring Mill Bread Co. in Washington, D.C., in 2004. Four year later, he met Kate, who had moved to D.C. to get her master's in art therapy. The two married and made the decision to move back to Kate's hometown to share their love of food and the arts with small batches of breads and sweets.

David Munro

Cooking has always been a passion for David Munro. Starting at the age of ten, weekends were spent with his Mum and Nan baking and learning, which taught him that the most important ingredient was love. This inspired David to a career in the culinary arts. He began his career in Kenilworth, England, which led him to the position of executive chef of the Clarendon House Hotel, before immigrating to the United States in 1991.

He has been fortunate to cook at many great restaurants, including the now closed Golden Mushroom in Southfield, Michigan. In 1998 another passion—beer—led to a slight career change. After working at the distributor level, David began working in sales as a regional representative at Bell's Brewery, the seventh-largest craft brewer in the United States, where skill, innovation, quality, and love go into every beer, just like a cookie. He now oversees draft field quality as part of Bell's key accounts team.

Roshi Muns

Roshi Muns is the founder and owner of Society Bakery in Dallas, Texas. Society Bakery was propelled into national recognition when Ellen DeGeneres and AOL named theirs one of the "Top Ten Cupcakes" in America. Since then, *People* magazine listed Society Bakery as one of "Four top bakeries in L.A., Dallas, Birmingham, and N.Y.C." Sherky's listed Society Bakery as one of "10 Bakeries You Need to Try Across the U.S." The Daily Meal also included them among the "Top 50 Cupcakes in America." Society Bakery has been seen on the Food Network, the Cooking Channel, and in *Bon Appétit* magazine. Society Bakery has had the honor of making sweets for numerous celebrities such as Billy Joel, Mark Cuban, Jerry Jones, Duff Goldman, Steven Tyler, Diddy, Grouplove, and New Kids on the Block.

In keeping with the bakery slogan of "Be good to your sweet tooth, be good to society," Roshi founded the bakery in 2003 with the intention of mixing three great passions: baking, creativity, and the desire to lead a meaningful life. Roshi named Society Bakery because she believes a business can be profitable and charitable at the same time. This has shaped how she has led the bakery to be involved in the local community by giving away thousands of cupcakes every year in exchange for items that local charities need. For more information, visit www.societybakery.com.

Brian Noyes
After twenty-five years as an art director with the *Washington Post*, *Preservation*, and *Smithsonian*, Brian Noyes left to launch a rural bakery in the Virginia Piedmont hunt country. He bought an old red farm truck from designer Tommy Hilfiger, baked out of his farmhouse, and sold pies, cakes, bread, granola, and cookies from the back of the truck. When Marian Burros of the *New York Times* discovered his pies and wrote about him in a holiday food story, his website hits went from two dozen to 57,000 in one day. The Red Truck Bakery was born, moved to a renovated 1921 Esso service station, and has received many national awards and honors from *Condé Nast Traveler* ("One of the 13 Sweetest Bakeries in America"), *Bon Appétit*, *Garden & Gun*, *Esquire*, *Southern Living*, and *Saveur* magazines. Everything is made by hand using only fresh, local, seasonal ingredients whenever possible, and hundreds of Red Truck Bakery moonshine cakes (with real Virginny hooch from the next county) are sent nationwide each year from www.redtruckbakery.com.

One Girl Cookies
Dave Crofton and his wife, Dawn Casale, opened their first One Girl Cookies bakery and café in Cobble Hill, Brooklyn, in 2005. They have been featured in *Fine Cooking*, *Gourmet*, *Food & Wine*, the *New York Times*, *Time Out New York*, *Bon Appétit*, *New York Magazine*, and *Martha Stewart Weddings*, as well as many other national publications. Their cookbook, *One Girl Cookies: Recipes for Cakes, Cupcakes, Whoopie Pies, and Cookies from Brooklyn's Beloved Bakery*, was released in January 2012.

Mandy Puntney
Mandy Puntney co-owns 4&20 Bakery and Café in Madison, Wisconsin, with her husband, Evan Dannells. For more information, visit their Facebook page at www.facebook.com/semperpie.

Alex Raij
Alex Raij is chef and owner, with husband Elder Montero, of El Comedor, El Quinto Pino, and Txikito in New York City and La Vara in Brooklyn. A graduate of the Culinary Institute of America, Raij was named *Eater*'s 2012 "Chef of the Year."

Steven Satterfield
Through his twenty years of experience in restaurants, chef Steven Satterfield has developed strong relationships with local farmers—a connection that came to fruition in his and co-owner Neal McCarthy's exciting restaurant venture, Miller Union. Named after the Miller Union Stockyards once located on the property, the restaurant inhabits a refurbished midcentury warehouse space in Atlanta's former West Side meatpacking district. Satterfield believes in an authentic approach to farmstead-inspired cooking. His trademark style is simple yet refined, and the dishes he creates focus on updated regional classics with fresh, produce-driven ideas.

A Georgia native, Satterfield is a leader in the progressive culinary community as an active member of Slow Food Atlanta, Georgia Organics, Community Farmer's Markets, Chefs Collaborative, and the Southern Foodways Alliance. He was also nominated for *Food & Wine* magazine's "People's Best New Chef," following Miller Union's placement on the "Best New Restaurants in America" lists from *Bon Appétit* and *Esquire*, as well as *Atlanta* magazine's "Restaurant of the Year." The James Beard Foundation chose Steven as a top five finalist for Best Chef: Southeast in 2013, 2014, and 2015. Miller Union was recognized as a semifinalist for the national award of Best New Restaurant in 2010.

Satterfield lives in the historic neighborhood of Inman Park in Atlanta. An avid cyclist, he also enjoys exploring the Georgia coast, listening to new music, teaching people to cook, and researching cocktails with the bartenders of Miller Union.

Carlene Schipfmann
Boulevard Brewing Company guest relations representative Carlene Schipfmann finds joy in experimenting with baked goods and unique ingredients, like beer. Carlene has been baking since she was in grade school, but really started getting into baking with beer, wine, and spirits over the past ten years. She has been part of the Boulevard tour experience for more than seven years. Boulevard Brewing Company has grown to become one of the largest specialty brewers in the Midwest, dedicated to the craft of producing fresh, flavorful beers using traditional ingredients and the best of both old and new brewing techniques. For more information, visit www.boulevard.com.

Emily Stone
After attending the California Culinary Academy in San Francisco, California, Emily relocated to the Pacific Northwest. She is now the head pastry chef at Pearl Bakery in Portland, Oregon. For more information, visit www.pearlbakery.com.

Stone Brewing Co.
Known for its bold, flavorful, and largely hop-centric beers, Stone Brewing Co. has been brewing in San Diego's North County since 1996. Founded by Greg Koch and Steve Wagner, Stone is the tenth-largest craft brewer in the United States. The company is dedicated to supporting the communities it serves and promoting a culture of social responsibility. In addition to brewing, Stone owns two eclectic farm-to-table restaurants—Stone Brewing World Bistro & Gardens, Escondido, and Stone Brewing World Bistro & Gardens, Liberty Station—as well as Stone Farms, an organic farm located near the brewery, which grows produce for the restaurants. For more information on Stone Brewing Co., please visit www.stonebrewing.com.

Sweetness Bake Shop & Café
With two locations and its Sugar Rush dessert truck, Sweetness Bake Shop & Café hits the spot with their creative combination of flavors, some of which are so unique, they've become synonymous with Miami. They have more than three hundred cupcake flavors, with ten different kinds available daily. Their signature desserts, including Maple Bacon Cupcakes, Cake n' Shakes, Guava & Passion Fruit Flan, and Key Lime Dessert Shots, support an ever-changing menu that also includes limited-edition and seasonal flavors.

Sweetness has been acclaimed by *Food & Wine* magazine as having one of the "Nation's Best New Cupcakes," and the *Miami New Times* named it "Miami's Best Bakery" in 2011.

Jeff Usinowicz

Jeff Usinowicz was raised in Montclair, New Jersey, and spent many of his childhood years enjoying the cuisine of New York City. After attending culinary school in Portland, Oregon, he returned to New York City and developed a love for Italian food while under Michael Romano at Union Square Café.

His career brought him to Portland, where he worked as the chef de cuisine at Laslow's Broadway Bistro. Following a tour as a corporate chef for NW Hayden Enterprises, where he helped build twenty new restaurants and concepts and consult on thirty more eateries, Jeff met up with the team at Deschutes Brewery. He built the brewery's kitchen and became the corporate executive chef. Jeff has found that cooking with beer is a huge new world he thoroughly enjoys and will continue to grow with for years to come.

William Werner

William Werner is chef/partner of Craftsman and Wolves, a contemporary patisserie in the vibrant Mission District of San Francisco, with an online retail shop and farmers' market stand at the venerable Ferry Plaza Farmers Market. Called "the most brilliant pastry shop in years" by Dana Cowin of *Food & Wine*, Craftsman and Wolves offers seasonally changing pastries, cakes, confections, confitures, breads, and desserts, as well as savory fare and signature drinks. Since opening, Werner has garnered praise both locally and nationally in publications including the *Wall Street Journal*, *Real Simple*, *Esquire*, and *Bon Appétit*, and *GQ* magazine named his famous "Rebel Within" as #6 on "The 50 Best Things to Eat and Drink Right Now."

Named *San Francisco* magazine's 2014 Best Pastry Chef, one of *Plate* magazine's 2014 "30 Chefs to Watch," Star Chefs' "2013 Rising Star Artisan," and a James Beard Foundation Outstanding Pastry Chef Award nominee, Werner also serves as a Valrhona pastry chef consultant, leading professional culinary demonstrations and classes in the United States and Canada. Recently, Werner collaborated with Self Edge co-owner Kiya Babzani and Darn-It! studio for a custom-designed Craftsman and Wolves denim apron, and with Etta+Billie owner Alana Rivera on a hand-crafted praline and burnt orange soap. In the early summer of 2015, Werner and team will open Craftsman and Wolves inside PLATFORM, a collection of art, fashion, and culinary talent at Hayden Tract in Los Angeles, California.

Nick Wesemann

Nick Wesemann grew up learning to make lemon meringue pies and cookies in the kitchen of his grandmother's bakery in Nevada, Missouri. He continued his education with the chef-apprenticeship program at Johnson County Community College, where he also earned a degree in food and beverage management. Wesemann became the pastry chef at The American Restaurant in Kansas City, Missouri, in 2006. In 2014 and 2015, he was named a semifinalist for the James Beard Foundation's Outstanding Pastry Chef Award.

Crystal Wiebe

Crystal Wiebe is a proud dog mom and craft beer lover. She's also the founder of Beer Paws, a company spawned by her need to find a reliable place to keep a bottle opener. After outfitting hundreds of dogs with bottle opener collar attachments, Beer Paws began partnering with breweries in the Kansas City area and Nebraska to turn spent grains into dog biscuits. Beer Paws is also the only Midwest maker of "beer" for dogs. The company donates a portion of all profits to animal rescue organizations. Miraculously, Crystal's dogs Coconut and Kona are not currently fat.

Chelsea Williams

Chelsea Williams has been baking for more than three decades. She's been a corporate pastry chef, and a lead baker and pastry chef for two natural food grocery chains, and has spent time as an organic farmer. She's currently the owner and operator of Chelsea's Bakehaus, which provides cookies and wholesome treats to coffee shops, natural grocers, and people.

Trey Winkle

Born and raised in Tulsa, Oklahoma, Trey Winkle is an avid homebrewer and craft beer lover, in addition to being the executive chef at the R Bar & Grill. He learned on the line and developed his minimalist cooking style as the former sous chef at Juniper and SoChey Jazz Cafe.

Forrest Wright

Forrest is the general manager and mind behind the menu at PT's Coffee, an internationally acclaimed coffee bar in Topeka, Kansas. Forrest breaks the convention of the average sandwich shop/bakery with inventive sweet and savory combinations and modern takes on high-end pastries, as well as a unique craft beer selection and cocktail menu. He strives to provide a decadent and creative culinary indulgence to the public while providing a quality service.

Molly Yeh

Molly Yeh is the voice behind the blog *My Name Is Yeh*, where she writes about moving from Brooklyn, New York, to live with her husband on a farm in North Dakota. A graduate of the Juilliard School, Yeh incorporates music, life, and food into her online chronicle, where she also shares recipes inspired by her Jewish and Asian roots.

ACKNOWLEDGMENTS

Books are lovely collaborations that bring all manner of collaborators into your life. The pairings are unexpected and delightful, kind of like the right cookie and beer.

This book wouldn't exist if Andrews McMeel Publishing's book division President and Publisher Kirsty Melville didn't reach out with the idea that pairing cookies and beer had the makings of a very fun project. My heart agreed with her. My arteries are still on the fence.

I'm thankful that I have an agent, Jonathan Lyons with Curtis Brown, who is thoughtful, considerate, and remarkably efficient at turning conversations into books on the shelf. I'm also grateful that so many chefs and bakers were open to sharing their recipes and talent. This book sings because of them. If it gets off-key, that's on me.

The Boulevard Brewing Co. opened up their tasting lab and more than a few bottles to help this book get off the ground.

Jocelyn Jacobson and her husband, Jake, were invaluable for their enthusiasm and assistance with recipe testing. I would not have crossed the finish line without them. Erin Brown at Dolce Bakery put deliciousness in every bite, and John Couture and the staff at Bier Station were essential for their beer knowledge and willingness to remain excited each time I placed a new Tupperware full of cookies on the bar. Baker Chelsea Williams produced beautiful cookies for the photo shoot that food stylist Trina Kahl handled with a deft hand and delightful humor. Photographer Lauren Frisch lent her talents, energy, and patience. Photographer Ron Berg and his team brought to life the joy of this book.

I could not have put *Cookies & Beer* together without the assistance of the entire team at Andrews McMeel. Creative Director Tim Lynch and Art Director Diane Marsh were incredibly open and dynamic. And I was lucky to have two editors, Julie Bunge and Jean Lucas, who were each willing to push themselves and me to ensure the book crackled. Copy Chief Maureen Sullivan made sure the reader (that's you) would be along for the ride. Andrea Shores is an outstanding publicist and advocate.

As always, I don't get to do what I do (and I love what I do) without my family. I've got some on the East and West Coasts and a bunch in the middle that know how to make it feel like home in Kansas City. To Abraham and Charlotte, thank you for rolling out dough balls and, occasionally, eating cookies or powdered sugar for dinner. To Kate, thanks for the support and love, which make me whole.

METRIC CONVERSIONS & EQUIVALENTS

METRIC CONVERSION FORMULAS

TO CONVERT	MULTIPLY
Ounces to grams	Ounces by 28.35
Pounds to kilograms	Pounds by .454
Teaspoons to milliliters	Teaspoons by 4.93
Tablespoons to milliliters	Tablespoons by 14.79
Fluid ounces to milliliters	Fluid ounces by 29.57
Cups to milliliters	Cups by 236.59
Cups to liters	Cups by .236
Pints to liters	Pints by .473
Quarts to liters	Quarts by .946
Gallons to liters	Gallons by 3.785
Inches to centimeters	Inches by 2.54

APPROXIMATE METRIC EQUIVALENTS

WEIGHT

¼ ounce	7 grams
½ ounce	14 grams
¾ ounce	21 grams
1 ounce	28 grams
1¼ ounces	35 grams
1½ ounces	42.5 grams
1⅔ ounces	45 grams
2 ounces	57 grams
3 ounces	85 grams
4 ounces (¼ pound)	113 grams
5 ounces	142 grams
6 ounces	170 grams
7 ounces	198 grams
8 ounces (½ pound)	227 grams
16 ounces (1 pound)	454 grams
35.25 ounces (2.2 pounds)	1 kilogram

VOLUME

¼ teaspoon	1 milliliter
½ teaspoon	2.5 milliliters
¾ teaspoon	4 milliliters
1 teaspoon	5 milliliters
1¼ teaspoons	6 milliliters
1½ teaspoons	7.5 milliliters
1¾ teaspoons	8.5 milliliters
2 teaspoons	10 milliliters
1 tablespoon (½ fluid ounce)	15 milliliters
2 tablespoons (1 fluid ounce)	30 milliliters
¼ cup	60 milliliters
⅓ cup	80 milliliters
½ cup (4 fluid ounces)	120 milliliters
⅔ cup	160 milliliters
¾ cup	180 milliliters
1 cup (8 fluid ounces)	240 milliliters
1¼ cups	300 milliliters
1½ cups (12 fluid ounces)	360 milliliters
1⅔ cups	400 milliliters
2 cups (1 pint)	460 milliliters
3 cups	700 milliliters
4 cups (1 quart)	0.95 liter
1 quart plus ¼ cup	1 liter
4 quarts (1 gallon)	3.8 liters

LENGTH

⅛ inch	3 millimeters
¼ inch	6 millimeters
½ inch	1¼ centimeters
1 inch	2½ centimeters
2 inches	5 centimeters
2½ inches	6 centimeters
4 inches	10 centimeters
5 inches	13 centimeters
6 inches	15¼ centimeters
12 inches (1 foot)	30 centimeters

COMMON INGREDIENTS
AND THEIR APPROXIMATE EQUIVALENTS
1 cup all-purpose flour = 140 grams
1 stick butter (4 ounces • ½ cup • 8 tablespoons) – 110 grams
1 cup butter (8 ounces • 2 sticks • 16 tablespoons) = 220 grams
1 cup brown sugar, firmly packed = 225 grams
1 cup granulated sugar = 200 grams

OVEN TEMPERATURES
To convert Fahrenheit to Celsius, subtract 32 from Fahrenheit, multiply the result by 5, then divide by 9.

DESCRIPTION	FAHRENHEIT	CELSIUS	BRITISH GAS MARK
Very cool	200°	95°	0
Very cool	225°	110°	¼
Very cool	250°	120°	½
Cool	275°	135°	1
Cool	300°	150°	2
Warm	325°	165°	3
Moderate	350°	175°	4
Moderately hot	375°	190°	5
Fairly hot	400°	200°	6
Hot	425°	220°	7
Very hot	450°	230°	8
Very hot	475°	245°	9

Information compiled from a variety of sources, including *Recipes into Type* by Joan Whitman and Dolores Simon (Newton, MA: Biscuit Books, 1993); *The New Food Lover's Companion* by Sharon Tyler Herbst (Hauppauge, NY: Barron's, 2013); and *Rosemary Brown's Big Kitchen Instruction Book* (Kansas City, MO: Andrews McMeel, 1998).

INDEX

One Barrel Brewing Company,
Commuter Kölsch, 70–71
One Girl Cookies, 64–65, 118
Orange & Ginger Spiced Cookies,
43–45
Oreos, 19
oversized wine glass, x
oyster stout, 40

P

packaged cookies and beer, 19
Pale Ale, 84–85. *See also*
American pale ale; English-
style pale ale; IPA
Pastaria, 42, 98–99
Patisserie 46, 76–78
Peach and Hefeweizen Jam Brown
Butter Thumbprint Cookies,
48–49
Peanut Butter Patties (Tagalongs),
40
Pearl Bakery, 22
Pearl Bakery Chocolate Chunk
Cookies, 26–27
pecans, 12–13
persimmons, 80–81
pilsner, x
pint glass, x
pinwheels, 19
Polvorones, 79
Port Brewing Company, Old
Viscosity Ale, 38–39
porters, x, 12–13, 19, 88–89. *See
also specific porters*
PT's Coffee, 50–51
Pumping Iron (Schwarzenegger),
vii
pumpkin
Pumpkin Butterscotch Cookies,
52–53
Pumpkin Chocolate Chip
Cookies, 46–47

Puntney, Mandy
background, 118
Peach and Hefeweizen Jam
Brown Butter Thumbprint
Cookies, 48–49

Q

quadrupel, x, 33
Bourbon Barrel Quad, 52–53

R

R Bar & Grill, 14–15
radlers, 8–9
Ginger Lemon Radler Cookies,
107–8
Raij, Alex
background of, 118
Polvorones, 79
Recommended Daily writing
project, viii
Red Truck Bakery, 74
Red Truck Bakery's Persimmon
Cookies, 80–81
The Reverend, viii, 33
Reynolds Buttercream Filling,
70–71
Rich Butter Cookies with Fennel
Seed and Sea Salt, 61–63
Rivera, Alana, 120
Robust Porter, 6–7
Romano, Michael, 120
Russian imperial stout, 46
Russian Tea Cakes, 82–83
Rye (restaurant), 75
rye IPA
Rye IPA Apricot Crumble Bars,
98–99
Rye Shortbread, 98–99

S

saison, 50–51, 107–8
Saison-Brett, 50–51
Samoas. *See* Caramel deLites

Samuel Smith, Oatmeal Stout, 3–5
Satterfield, Steven
background of, 118–19
Chocolate-Almond-Coconut
Macaroons, 33
savory cookies, 60
Batch Bakehouse's Vanilla Basil
Shortie, 70–71
Chai Spice, 68–69
Curry Coconut Macaroons,
66–67
Olive Oil & Almond Biscotti,
64–65
Rich Butter Cookies with
Fennel Seed and Sea Salt,
61–63
Schipfmann, Carlene
background, 119
Ginger Lemon Radler Cookies,
107–8
Schwarzenegger, Arnold, vii
scotch ale, 40
Serious Eats, 34–37
shortbread
Bacon Shortbread Cookies, 8–9
Batch Bakehouse's Vanilla Basil
Shortie, 70–71
Chocolate-Covered Caramel-
Filled Shortbread Cookies,
34–37
Maple Fig Shortbread Cookies,
50–51
Rye IPA Apricot Crumble Bars,
98–99
Shortbread (Trefoils), 40
Sierra Nevada Brewing Company,
Pale Ale, 84–85
slender cylinder, x
Smoked Porter, 23–25, 100–101
snifter, x
Society Bakery, 84–85

Andrews McMeel Publishing, LLC
an Andrews McMeel Universal company
1130 Walnut Street, Kansas City, Missouri 64106

www.andrewsmcmeel.com

14 15 16 17 18 SDB 10 9 8 7 6 5 4 3 2 1

ISBN: 978-1-4494-7088-3

Library of Congress Control Number: 2015931598

Photographer: Ron Berg
Photography by Lauren Frisch Pusateri: pages iv, vi, xii,
27, 29, 47, 53, 57, 67, 72, 85, 89, 101, 116
Food Stylist: Trina Kahl
Cookies baked courtesy of Chelsea Williams
Glassware courtesy of Bier Station
Editors: Jean Lucas, Julie Bunge
Designer: Diane Marsh
Creative Director: Tim Lynch
Production Editor: Maureen Sullivan
Production Manager: Carol Coe
Demand Planner: Sue Eikos

ATTENTION: SCHOOLS AND BUSINESSES
Andrews McMeel books are available at quantity discounts with bulk
purchase for educational, business, or sales promotional use. For information,
please e-mail the Andrews McMeel Publishing Special Sales Department:
specialsales@amuniversal.com.